# SAVE ONE
## THE RIPPLE EFFECT

*For those touched by a loved one's abortion*

### SHEILA HARPER

Copyright 2023 by Sheila Harper. All rights reserved.

No part of this publication may be reproduced or transmitted in any form or by any means, mechanical or electronic, including photocopying and recording, or by any information storage and retrieval system, without permission in writing from the authors or publisher (except by a reviewer, who may quote brief passages and/or show brief video clips in a review).

Disclaimer:
The Publisher and Authors make no representations or warranties with respect to the accuracy or completeness of the contents of this work and specifically disclaim all warranties, including without limitation warranties of fitness for a particular purpose. No warranty may be created or extended by sales or promotional materials. The advice and strategies contained herein may not be suitable for every situation. This work is sold with the understanding that the Authors are not engaged in rendering legal, counseling, or other professional services. If professional assistance is required, the services of a competent professional person should be sought. Neither the Publisher nor the Authors shall be liable for damages arising here from. The fact that an organization or website, or book, is referred to in this work as a citation and/or a potential source of further information does not mean that the Authors or the Publisher endorses the information the organization or website may provide or recommendations it may make. Further, readers should be aware that the Internet websites listed in this work may have changed or disappeared between when this work was written and when it is read.

**ISBN: 979-8-9880079-1-3**

Unless otherwise noted, all Scripture quotations are taken from the *New Living Translation (NLT)*, copyright 1996, Tyndale House Publishers, Inc.

Cover and interior layout by 2Binc Creative, LLC at 2BincCreative.com in Onsted, Michigan.

*Credit: Cover paintography by LUMEZIA at iStock by Getty Images.*

## DEDICATION

*To the family member or friend reading this book:*
*Your loss is real, it is valid, and it's worthy to be discussed.*
*Thank you for having the courage to come forward and deal*
*with the pain of a loved one's abortion.*

*And to my family members whose profound loss*
*of my daughter is felt every day.*

# TABLE OF CONTENTS

Read First ........................................................................... 6

Acknowledgments ............................................................ 7

Praise .................................................................................. 8

Introduction ...................................................................... 11

A Message from God ....................................................... 15

CHAPTER 1 - Your Source of Courage ........................ 17

CHAPTER 2 - What Happened to Me? ....................... 33

CHAPTER 3 - Dealing with Stray Emotions: Part I ... 53

CHAPTER 4 - Dealing with Stray Emotions: Part II .. 73

CHAPTER 5 - Forgiving Others ..................................... 89

CHAPTER 6 - God's Grace .............................................. 103

CHAPTER 7 - Can I Forgive Myself? ............................ 113

CHAPTER 8 - Renewing Your Mind ............................ 125

CHAPTER 9 - Who Is This Child? ................................. 137

CHAPTER 10 - Brothers of Courage ............................ 149

In Conclusion .................................................................... 165

Other Books by the Harpers .......................................... 167

# READ FIRST

This is a very personal journey for you, and we want to help you through it. If you purchased this book to complete on your own, we would love the chance to travel this journey with you. Please contact the SaveOne staff through the website below, and we will confidentially complete this study by your side or find a local chapter near you.

If you are exploring this book to teach this study at your church or pregnancy center, we would love to get to know you better. You hold in your hands a book that could transform the men and women in your community, helping them become the mothers, fathers, wives, husbands, and leaders they were called to be before this choice entered their lives. Please email our office, and we will help you every step of the way.

We give support by offering a free web page so those who come to our site can contact your church or center directly. You will also have a SaveOne chapter coordinator in your state as the point of contact. We offer training several different ways, plus prayer support, and regular follow-up and updates. We are here to help you help others to freedom.

saveone.org • info@saveone.org

# ACKNOWLEDGMENTS

First of all, to my Lord and Savior, Jesus Christ, thank you for paying the price for my sins. Thank you for saving me, restoring me, loving me first, and using me as a vessel to bring your restoration to others.

Thank you to my husband, Jack, the first person who had the bright idea for me to stop waiting on someone else to write this study and for me to do it. You are a wonderful editor, and I love you.

Thanks to Christina Brocato. I couldn't have completed this book without your expertise.

Thanks to my BFFs: While dealing with such a heavy subject, you guys always have, and are still providing my comic relief.

# PRAISE

"The best part of having SaveOne at North Little Rock First Assembly is not only seeing these men and women freed from years of bondage but others in our congregation seeing this and realizing they too can deal with any hurt and pain in their pasts."

Pastor Rod Loy
North Little Rock First Assembly, North Little Rock, AR

"SaveOne is an incredible ministry that brings healing after the heartbreak of abortion to both women and men. SaveOne, under the leadership of founders Jack and Sheila Harper, offers resources that walk the broken through to a place of complete healing and new life. SaveOne shines a beacon of light, dispelling the lies that have reigned in the darkness. Through the powerful, effective curriculum shared through chapters in the local church, SaveOne walks men and women out of brokenness into healing and strength, allowing God's joy to overcome sorrow.

If you have ten or more people in your church or on your team, you need this resource. Abortion has pervaded every area and status, regardless of religious affiliation. While we work tirelessly to eliminate abortions in our nation, we need to work lovingly and diligently to heal those wounded by it. Compassionately step in and start a SaveOne chapter in your church and give to the ministry. Pray for those fighting this battle in the spirit while they lovingly reach those in need of healing. Together, we can push back the darkness and accomplish a significant work for eternity!"

Kay Burnett
Former Director, National Women's Dept. for the Assemblies of God

"SaveOne is an absolutely vital ministry to men and women who suffer from the psychological after-effects of abortion. Their resources are second to none! Excellence is their hallmark. I highly recommend this wonderful organization."

Bradley Mattes
Executive Director Life Issues Institute

"SaveOne has had an immeasurable impact upon our cities of Shreveport and Bossier. The silent holocaust of abortion has an adversary in this anointed ministry. In my opinion, there is no more powerful voice for the unborn."

Pastor Denny Duron
Shreveport Community Church Shreveport, LA

"I have known Sheila Harper and her family for many years and have seen God use them in so many ways. One of those ways is the ministry of SaveOne. SaveOne is reaching out to those who have experienced or been affected by the pain of abortion. This ministry is a great way to impact those in your church and community with a message of grace and hope. I fully endorse and recommend SaveOne to every church!"

Pastor John McKinzie
Lead Pastor Hope Fellowship Frisco, TX

# INTRODUCTION

I walked but didn't know if my legs would carry me. I was terrified, not knowing what to expect. This was the last thing on earth I ever wanted or expected to do. I was only nineteen… How would I explain this to my parents? I thought I could just get this "problem" taken care of and not ever have to think about it again. I couldn't have been more wrong.

I signed in and was told I would receive counseling. My mind went wild thinking of how grateful I was that someone in charge was actually going to counsel me. I knew I needed to talk to someone who could give me an alternative, someone who didn't have all this craziness going on in her head like I did.

I was called into the office, where a cold, emotionless woman behind a desk met me. I immediately burst into tears. I thought this would be my chance to describe what I was feeling, and someone would help me.

The woman simply asked, "Do you want to have this abortion?" I told her through my sobs, "I don't know any other choice." She wrote a number 2 on a small white card, handed it to me, and said, "Okay, then go sit in the waiting room, and they'll call your number in a minute."

I was devastated. At that moment, I realized counseling was the last thing they were going to give me. I was nothing but 250 bucks to them. By the time my number was called, the room was filled to capacity, mostly with young girls just like me. They were lined around the walls, sitting on couches, chairs, and the floor. I stepped my way over and around them and entered an adjoining room. I lay down on the table and offered my first child to these strangers.

The procedure was excruciatingly painful and an experience I will never forget. When I walked out of the abortion clinic that day, I was changed forever. How much I had changed was yet to be revealed.

The book you hold in your hands is what God gave me to help people find the emotional, mental, and spiritual healing they need after a loved one's abortion. There is not one person alive who grows up thinking someday he or she wants to be involved in an abortion. You might not have learned about the abortion until years later, or you may have driven your sister or friend to the clinic. Either way, if you have any form of regret or grief, this book is for you.

I realize not everyone suffers in the same way after an abortion. Depending on your level of involvement, some people have no lingering feelings of shame or regret, and for that, I'm thankful. But others spend their entire lives trying to condone the choice they made, punishing themselves, refusing to forgive themselves, or thinking God is punishing them. They often have survivor's guilt, asking the question of how life might have been different had this child lived.

This book was written to help you take this mantle from around your neck and lay it down. You've been carrying it around way too long. I'm here as an example of God's Grace and just how far it extends. After years of punishing myself with drugs, alcohol, a suicide attempt, and other things, I finally completed a study much like this one that liberated me after seven years of horrible emotional bondage.

This study can do the same for you. You may have paid for an abortion or be a surviving sibling. Whatever the form of your loss, set your mind right now, to complete this study. There might be days you think this isn't worth the pain and memories you must endure, but I encourage you to stick it out and look really hard for the light at the end of the tunnel.

As you progress through each chapter, the light will grow brighter and more noticeable until one day, you wake up and find yourself standing in that light. I promise. I hope one day we will meet, and you can tell me the story of when the Light showed Himself to you.

While you're going through this book, I ask that you not jump ahead. There might be things in a later chapter that you are not ready for, and you might think you could never do. Not to worry; all you have to do is work through one chapter at a time. Each week, focus on that one chapter and nothing else. This way, by the time you get to later chapters, you will be ready to handle those things. Now that you're ready to get started, I want to say a prayer for you:

*Heavenly Father,*
*I come to you today and ask for your amazing grace to cover the person holding this book. You know the grief they bear. You know the choices they have made. I ask that you walk with them, Father, through the next few weeks as they progress through this study. You designed this book just for them, in fact, you had them in mind when you created this book. For that, I'm thankful.*

*Reveal your true self to her in a way she has never experienced. Let them know their pain is not too much for you to bear. You have called us to lay our cares on you and you will give us rest. That's what they need Lord, rest from this burden they were never intended to bear.*

*I thank you in advance for what you're going to do in this person's life. I've seen your miracles work in even the toughest cases. None are too big for you.*

*In Jesus' name, I pray, Amen.*

# A MESSAGE FROM GOD

## A MESSAGE FROM GOD

*My Child,*
*Your struggle has been long. Your heartache has been heavy. You have cried and questioned and laid your heart on the altar of sorrows.*

*I have been here with you through it all, as I will always be with you. But I am asking you today to make this choice: the choice to go on. For it is a choice in the end that only you can make—a choice to walk in the land of the living, to feel the sunshine and smile at the children, to be alive! A choice to believe that in spite of your loss and all it has cost you, there is much beauty and joy just outside your heart, waiting to be invited in.*

*I have good plans for you, my child, if only you will choose to embrace them. They are plans rich with a new hope and a good future. There are people I love out there in that place called "the future." People who need what only you can give them—your smile, your wisdom, your comfort, your personality.*

*Will you trust me to lead you to that good place? We will travel there together, one step at a time. I will be right beside you. Will you choose life?*

*Your loving Father, God.*

# CHAPTER 1
## *Your Source of Courage*

Verse to memorize this week:
*Give all your worries and cares to God, for
He cares about what happens to you.*

**1 Peter 5:7 NLT**

How do you picture God? As a little old man with a long white beard sitting in a rocking chair? As a huge, scary, mean man standing up in Heaven with bolts of lightning in each hand just waiting to zap you when you mess up? Or as your loving creator?

> *Disregard the study of God, and you sentence yourself to stumble and blunder through life blindfolded, as it were, with no sense of direction.*
>
> *J. I. Packer*

Whatever your perception is, we will spend this chapter finding out if it is correct.

**Describe how you picture God at this moment:**

_____
_____
_____
_____

**Do you feel this is an accurate portrayal?**

_____
_____
_____
_____

**Why or why not?**

_____
_____
_____
_____

Did you know that God is your protector, provider, hope, healer, father, and strength? He is able to see all that happens to you. He is able to calm any storm in your life. He is able to be there even when your friends and family aren't. He is able to give you a destiny. He is able to plan your future. He is able to open every door to get you to that future. He is able to put you back on the right path, even when you've chosen the wrong one. He is able to forgive you of your sins. He is able to send His very Son to die for you in order for that to happen. He is able to love you more than anyone on this earth has the capability to love. He is able to save your soul.

> *God's character does not change. Strain or shock can alter the character of a man, but nothing can alter the character of God.*
>
> *J. I. Packer*
> *Knowing God*

This is the kind of God that created you. His name is Yahweh, the great I AM. When He appeared to Moses at the burning bush **(Exodus 3:1–14)**, that is who He said He was. He is never changing. That is why He can describe Himself as I AM, and we cannot. We are always changing: I am sad, I am hungry, I am happy. God isn't like that. His mood doesn't change with the season. He said, "I AM," and that is who He is.

**As you were reading the preceding text describing who God is and what He is able to do, did you have a connection with one of those scenarios? If so, which one?**

_____

_____

_____

_____

_____

**Read Genesis 16:13 and Psalm 10:14. Does it comfort you or unsettle you to think God sees all? Why or why not?**

_____

_____

_____

_____

**Read Psalm 107:28-30. Does it comfort you or unsettle you to think God can calm any storm in your life? Why?**

_____

_____

_____

_____

**Read Hebrews 13:5 and Deuteronomy 31:6. What do these verses tell you about God being there for you?**

_____

_____

_____

_____

**Is there something you need that you feel God can't provide for you? If so, what is that need?**

_____

_____

_____

_____

**Read Psalm 91. What does that chapter mean to "you"?**

_____

_____

_____

_____

Now, **read Psalm 91** again, out loud, and in place of the word "you," say the word "me, my, or I." Can you see how God will protect you? The first verse states, "You shall dwell in the secret place of the most high." It is saying you have an intimate place of divine protection, and no threat can ever overpower God. **Verses 14-16** are God Himself speaking to you, telling you of the blessing He gives to those who know and love Him. Read this chapter often to remind you of God's protection.

We are so limited in our human bodies—by life, age, weather patterns, wealth (or lack of it), social status, emotional baggage, our families, ideas that have been formed for us by our families, self-esteem, our government... the list goes on and on.

> *God never changes moods, cools off in His affections, or loses enthusiasm.*
>
> *A.W. Tozer*

Do you realize God has no limits? He doesn't have an earthly body that ages and will eventually wear out. He isn't affected by weather patterns; He creates them. He doesn't care how much money you have or don't have; He is able to provide more or take away. He isn't impressed with your social status; He is the King of all Kings. He is saddened by the emotional baggage we carry; He wishes we would give it all to Him to carry. He hopes every day that we will begin to see ourselves as He sees us, not as our families or others tell us we are.

**Describe your relationship with God:**

_____
_____
_____
_____
_____
_____

**Read Psalm 139: 1-12. How do these verses explain the presence of God?**

_____
_____
_____
_____

**Do you believe He is this active in your life? Why or why not?**

_____
_____
_____
_____

God is as close to you as you will allow Him to be. He created you for a purpose, with a destiny. There is a song written that says, "There's a God-shaped hole in all of us." I love that word picture. Many of us work to fill that hole with work, material things, friends, relationships, drugs, sex, and/or alcohol. I'm sure you could add your own "fillers" to that list. But the truth is, until you fill that hole with an intimate relationship with God, you will constantly be searching, never feeling truly satisfied. He wants you to come to Him with your burdens.

**Read Jeremiah 29:11 and write it below:**

_____
_____
_____

**Do you believe this promise is for you?**

_____
_____
_____

**Write in your own words what this verse says to you:**

_____
_____
_____

**Read Jeremiah 29:12 through the first sentence of 14. There are three things He calls us to do in these verses. What are they?**

1. _____
2. _____
3. _____

**If we do these three things, what does He say He will do?**

_____
_____

God's destiny for you never included being involved in an abortion nor having the circumstances of one thrust upon you. When your loved one chose to take a left fork onto the road called Abortion, he or she veered off into an area that wasn't part of God's plan. Unfortunately, many times our families suffer the aftermath of being on that road as well. He wants to steer you back onto the road He created for you. He wants to take this experience and turn it into something beautiful for Him. Only God can do that, and He will if you allow Him.

**Read Genesis 50:20.** This verse tells you that what Satan means for evil in your life, God can turn to good.

> *I started this Bible study to try to help my mother, who has not moved forward with her life in many ways since her abortion; but quickly realized that I needed to surrender my grief for my baby sister to Jesus as well, and SaveOne has helped me do that.*
>
> *"Jackie"*
> *in SaveOne class*

**Do you believe God can do this in your life? Why or why not?**
_____
_____

**What do you feel your part in this procedure will be?**
_____
_____

**What steps can you take this week to get this process started?**
_____
_____

**1 Samuel 16:7** says, "For the Lord does not see as man sees; for man looks at the outward appearance, but the Lord looks at the heart." God knows your heart. He knows your sorrow. He knows any regret you may carry for your involvement in the abortion. He knows the hurt you feel for the loss you have endured. He has seen how you have tried to deal with this on your own for so long.

Now that you are dealing with the past, it's not a shock or a surprise to Him. He is happy that you have chosen to lay this burden down at this time in your life. These next few weeks are between you and only Him.

> *Our God is a God who not merely restores but takes up our mistakes and follies into His plan for us and brings good out of them. This is part of the wonder of his gracious sovereignty.*
>
> *J.I. Packer*

**Write your memory verse in the space below:**

_____

_____

_____

_____

Take a moment and think about the time period between when the abortion took place and today. Can you think of some instances in which God was active in your life? **Write them below:**

_____

_____

_____

_____

**Do you believe God loves you? Why or why not?**

_____

_____

_____

**If you believe God doesn't love you, explain what you believe you would have to do to get God to love you again:**

_____
_____
_____
_____

**Read Romans 8:35-39. What can separate the love of God from you?**

_____
_____
_____
_____

The New Living Translation says it best, I believe: "No, despite all these things, overwhelming victory is ours through Christ, who loved us. And I am convinced that nothing can ever separate us from His love. Death can't, and life can't. The angels can't, and the demons can't. Our fears for today, our worries about tomorrow, and even the powers of hell can't keep God's love away. Whether we are high above the sky or in the deepest ocean, nothing in all creation will ever be able to separate us from the love of God that is revealed in Christ Jesus our Lord." **Romans 8:37-39 NLT**

> *All my days I have been aware of One going before me and with me, of doors ajar that I never could have opened.*
>
> Vance Havner

I believe that has to be one of the most beautiful scriptures in the entire Bible. Nowhere does it say, "But if you have an abortion experience in your life, God will not take you back or love you anymore." No, it says **nothing** can separate us from His love.

**Now read Psalm 30. Write in your own words what you believe this Psalm means:**

_____

_____

_____

Stop for a minute. Put down this book, close your eyes, and picture yourself with one of those heavy, wooden yokes around your neck. Imagine how your body has become, carrying that yoke of abortion grief for as long as you've been carrying it. Now picture God reaching down and breaking it,

> *Courage is the power to let go of the familiar.*
>
> *Maury Davis*

crushing it. There isn't even a piece left that you could hold in your fingertips. It's just dust lying at your feet. Give this yoke to God right now. We must allow God to destroy the yoke of unresolved grief so it can never resume its previous position.

**Read Isaiah 10:27. What does this verse say God will do for you?**

_____

_____

Throughout this chapter, you have looked up many scriptures regarding who God is. This is by no means an exhaustive study, but it should give you some idea of who God can be and wants to be in your life.

Let's review. Look back at the beginning of this chapter and read your description of how you picture God. **Is that still an accurate portrayal?**

_____

_____

**Does that portrayal line up with the scriptures you have read?**

_____
_____
_____

**Can you start to see God as who the Bible says He is?**

_____
_____
_____

As you close this chapter, take a moment to pray and ask God to reveal Himself to you as the loving creator He really is.

**Write your prayer below:**

_____
_____
_____

**Write your scripture memory verse for the week:**

_____
_____
_____

**What knowledge did you gain from working through this chapter?**

_____
_____
_____

**What steps can you take this week to put this knowledge into practice?**

_____
_____
_____
_____

Please use the blank pages that follow to write the thoughts you are having about this book. What are you feeling, thinking, and going through? This may not be comfortable for you, but just try it. There is something about writing these things out on paper that frees you. You will have room to write down your thoughts at the end of each chapter.

*"Abortion teaches children that they have worth because they were conceived in the right conditions and at the right time; that they have value because their parents want them. Up to 50% of all American children have lost a brother or a sister to abortion, making it much more likely that they live with a performance view of love: I was born because I was wanted, therefore I better perform so they will continue to love me."*

Source:
https://www.nationalrighttolifenews.org/2015/02/the-suffering-brothers-and-sisters-of-aborted-children-2/

## JOURNAL PAGE

# JOURNAL PAGE

# CHAPTER 2
## What Happened to Me?

Verse to memorize this week:
*Then Jesus said, 'Come to me all of you who
are weary and carry heavy burdens, and I will give you rest.*

**Matthew 11:28 NLT**

The following comes from a journal written by Oswald Chambers. I include it here because I feel this writing is especially relevant for the men and women I talk to dealing with regret and shame from their abortion. Please read these words and remember your loved one and how they are coping with their decision to abort.

"It is possible for people to become so accustomed to their bondage they resist efforts to free them. The Hebrews had been slaves in Egypt for four hundred years. Slavery meant they were not free to do God's will or go where they wanted. Moses had come to tell the Israelites how they could experience freedom, yet they were more concerned about the reaction of their taskmasters than they were about pleasing God. For them to be free would mean that the pharaoh they were serving would be angry! It would mean that the Egyptians they had served all their lives might attack them. Freedom from their slavery did not seem to be worth the hardships they would inevitably endure." —Oswald Chambers

When God sets out to free us, there will often be a price we will have to pay. Grief can be a terrible form of bondage, yet we can become comfortable with it. We can grow so comfortable with fear that we don't know how to live without it. We can also grow comfortable with looking at our loved ones through the filter of abortion. As destructive as our sinful habits and lifestyle might be, we may prefer living with the familiar rather than being freed to experience the unknown. We may recognize the harmful influence of a friend but choose to reject God's will rather than offend our friend.

As incredible as it seems, the Israelites were angry with Moses for disrupting the life of slavery to which they had grown accustomed.

Have you been lulled into a comfortable relationship with your bondage?

Do you fear change more than you fear God? Are you willing to allow God to do what is necessary to free you?

When the children of Israel left Egypt after years of slavery, they took forty years to complete an eleven-day journey. Why did that happen? They were stuck in a rut. God wanted to take them to a place of great abundance and victory, but they couldn't conceive God's plan. They had believed for so long that they would never see this place. In their minds, life didn't exist beyond their slavery. Instead of having faith in God to take them to this new place, they focused on their problems.

> *Many of life's failures are people who did not realize how close they were to success when they gave up.*
>
> *Thomas Edison*

**Read Deuteronomy 1:6.** God was telling them they had dwelled way too long at this one place. He was trying to motivate them to move forward and get on with their lives. The fact you are using this book is proof that you know God has brought you to this place to tell you the same thing. You have suffered long enough at this mountain in your life. It's time to allow Him to take you to a greater place of abundance. For this to happen, you must take the limits off God and raise your level of expectancy. That means you can spend the next several weeks believing God is who He said He is, and He will do what He says He will do.

**Read Isaiah 61:7.** The NLT says, "Instead of shame and dishonor, you will inherit a double portion of prosperity and everlasting joy." God will pay you back double, but He can't do this unless you go into this believing there is more for you.

Don't accept this bondage any longer. Don't live in mediocrity. Set a new standard for your life. Take the limits off God and allow Him to take the limits off your life. Step out in faith and believe God is about to do a great thing.

Throughout this chapter, you will answer questions and remember details surrounding the abortion. You may be grieving personally from the loss of a niece or grandchild or the actions of a family member because of this loss. Regardless of the reason you are working through this study,

> *Everything that is done in the world is done by hope.*
>
> *Martin Luther*

please answer the questions about yourself. You may ask, "Why do I need to do this part?" The answer is sometimes, when we go through or find out about a traumatic experience for someone we love, we tend to exaggerate some details when remembering them. At other times we will forget details entirely because they are too painful to remember.

Whether this abortion experience was thirty years ago or one month ago, there might be details your mind has skewed as a protective device. To deal with this information properly, you will need to bring these memories out of the shadows and into the light, where you can see them truthfully.

None of these questions are meant to judge you or your loved one or make you feel badly, but only to help you remember. So please answer in as much detail as you can. Remember this, the answers to these questions are for your eyes only. Don't answer them according to how you think they should be answered but answer the questions as truthfully as you can remember. This exercise is to help you recall the details, even though they may be painful. I encourage you to do this so you can deal with them and get on with your life.

**How old were you when you found out about the pregnancy?**

_____

**Where were you living? (city, state)**

_____

**Were you working at the time? If so, where?**
_____
_____

**Were you told about the pregnancy before the abortion?**
_____
_____

**How did you feel when you found out about the pregnancy? Explain.**
_____
_____
_____

**How many abortions have happened around you that you are grieving?**
*(If more than one, we suggest you go through this study concentrating on only one at a time. Please feel free to talk to your teacher more about this if you have any questions.)*
_____
_____
_____

**Was God a part of your life during this time?**
_____
_____
_____

**Who was the father of the child, and how old was he?**
_____

**Were you related to him, or was he a friend? If he was a friend, how did you meet him?**
_____
_____
_____

**Did you talk to him about the pregnancy? If so, how did he react?**
_____
_____
_____
_____

**How did his reaction affect you?**
_____
_____
_____

**Who was the mother of the child, and how old was she?**
_____

**Were you related to her, or was she a friend? If she was a friend, how did you meet her?**
_____
_____
_____

**Did you talk to her about the pregnancy? If so, how did she react?**

_____
_____
_____
_____
_____

> *If you run into a wall, don't turn around and give up. Figure out how to climb it, go through it, or work around it.*
>
> *Michael Jordan*

**How did her reaction affect you?**

_____
_____
_____

**Who did you believe you couldn't tell about the pregnancy? Why?**

_____
_____
_____
_____

**Did the mother or father consider any alternatives to abortion? If so, what were they?**

_____
_____
_____
_____

**Why did they believe these alternatives weren't viable options?**

_____

_____

**Were you or anyone else involved in the decision process? If so, who?**

_____

_____

**Did you encourage either of them to have an abortion? If so, how do you feel about that decision now?**

_____

_____

**Did anyone encourage the mother or father to have an abortion? If so, who?** (List if more than one):

_____

_____

_____

**What are your feelings toward the people (or persons) today who might have encouraged the abortion?**

_____

_____

_____

**Did anyone encourage the mother or father to keep the child? If so, who?** (List if more than one):

_____

_____

**What are your feelings toward this person (or persons) today?**

_____
_____
_____
_____
_____
_____

> *When you get into a tight place and everything goes against you, till it seems as though you could not hang on a minute longer, never give up then, for that is just the place and time that the tide will turn.*
>
> *Harriet Beecher Stowe*

**How much time went by between finding out about the pregnancy and having your abortion experience?**

_____
_____
_____

**How far along was the pregnancy at the time of abortion?**

_____

**Did you take your loved one to the abortion facility or participate in the abortion in any way? If so, how?**

_____
_____
_____
_____
_____

**If you took your loved one, do you remember any of the people who worked at the facility? If so, who?**

_____
_____
_____
_____

**Is there anything that someone said to you while you were there that you've always remembered? If so, what?**

_____
_____
_____
_____

**If your friend or loved one had a chemical abortion, were you present during the process?**

_____
_____
_____
_____

**Is there anything someone said to you during the chemical abortion process that you've always remembered? If so, what?**

_____
_____
_____
_____

**Describe your feelings right before the abortion.**

_____
_____
_____
_____

**Describe your feelings right after the abortion.**

_____
_____
_____
_____

**What details, if any, do you remember from the abortion procedure?**

_____
_____
_____
_____

**What was your relationship with the mother or father of the child like after the abortion?**

_____
_____
_____
_____

**Do you have contact with the mother or father of the child now? Is it a good relationship?**
_____
_____
_____

**Did the abortion change your relationship? If so, how?**
_____
_____
_____

**What lasting effects has the abortion left you with mentally?**
_____
_____
_____

**What lasting effects has the abortion left you with emotionally?**
_____
_____
_____

**What lasting effects has the abortion left you with spiritually?**
_____
_____
_____

**Do you feel anger toward anyone from the abortion experience? If so, explain:**

_____
_____
_____
_____

**Do you feel bitterness toward anyone from that period of your life? If so, explain:**

_____
_____
_____
_____

**Have you experienced any long periods of depression? If so, explain:**

_____
_____
_____
_____

**What is your reaction when someone mentions the subject of abortion to you?**

_____
_____
_____
_____

**Are you able to talk about abortion without having a strong emotional reaction?**

_____
_____
_____
_____

**How do you feel when you are around babies or small children?**

_____
_____
_____
_____

**Think of all the responsibilities and activities in your life. Is there anything you are doing to try to pay for any involvement you had in the abortion? If so, what?**

_____
_____
_____
_____

**Have you in the past, or do you presently have nightmares or dreams that you believe stem from the abortion? If so, explain:**

_____
_____
_____
_____

**Have you done anything in the past, or are you currently doing anything, to punish yourself for your abortion? If so, explain:**

_____
_____
_____
_____
_____

> *God collects our tears as precious memories. He holds these precious memories as a sign of His presence with us in our darkest hours.*
>
> *Jack Harper*
> *SaveOne Men's Director*

**Did you begin to use drugs and alcohol, or did you increase the amounts after the abortion? If so, explain:**

_____
_____
_____
_____

**What was your perception of God at the time of your abortion?**

_____
_____
_____
_____

**Did that perception change afterward? If so, explain:**

_____
_____
_____

**Have you ever contemplated or attempted suicide? If so, explain:**

_____
_____
_____
_____
_____
_____

> *Prayer is not asking. Prayer is putting oneself in the hands of God, at His disposition, and listening to His voice in the depth of our hearts.*
>
> *Mother Teresa*

**How could the knowledge you have gained about abortion be used to help others?**

_____
_____
_____
_____

**What do you hope to gain by completing this book?**

_____
_____
_____
_____

After writing your answer to the last question, say it out loud. Now say a short prayer to God, asking Him to help you gain what you want to gain by completing this book.

**Write your prayer below:**

_____
_____
_____
_____
_____

**What knowledge did you gain from working through this chapter?**

_____
_____
_____

**What steps can you take this week to put that knowledge into practice?**

_____
_____
_____

**Write your scripture memory verse for the week:**

_____
_____
_____

Now that you have finished answering all these questions, perhaps you have remembered more than I have asked about. On the following pages, write any details you have remembered, then go back over the questions and add anything you deem necessary to your answers.

Below is a letter written by my sister Sonja and used with her permission. These are hard words for me to read but necessary words to speak. Families **DO** hurt after abortion.

*I had not even heard of anyone getting an abortion until you did. I had heard of abortion but hadn't given it much thought. I remember you, and I went to dinner, and you told me. My first thought was, "that was my niece or nephew." My heart just ached, and I wasn't even sure why. I remember wondering why you didn't come to me earlier so I could have helped you through it, but you had already done it, and there was nothing left for me to do but hear you out.*

*I remember that on my way home, I felt like I had been kicked in the gut and still didn't know why it affected me that way. It never changed how much I loved you; it just made me very, very sad for days. We didn't have the Internet then, so I got a book on abortion, and after that, I knew why it made me sad.*

*I kept my distance from you for a while, just simply because I wasn't sure how to handle it. I had to get my head around it but keep showing you love and understanding, and it just wasn't an easy time. I loved you so much I wanted to just hold you, yet I was so mad at you I didn't want to see you. For sure, I had to turn to God for help.*

*I never told you any of this because I didn't want to make you feel worse. I prayed for you ALOT even when we didn't see things eye to eye. Back then, I knew my words could hurt you, and I couldn't find healing words for a long time. I'm glad now that the Lord has healed you and US, and it's helped knowing there have been thousands of babies saved from that tragedy through that healing.*

*I love you.*

# JOURNAL PAGE

## JOURNAL PAGE

# CHAPTER 3
## *Dealing With Stray Emotions: Part I*

Verse to memorize this week:
*Be anxious for nothing, but in everything by prayer and supplication, with thanksgiving, let your requests be made known to God; and the peace of God, which surpasses all understanding, will guard your hearts and minds through Christ Jesus.*

**Philippians 4:6, 7**

When a person experiences a trauma, such as abortion, each individual deals with that trauma in different ways. Often times there is a chronic inability to process the painful thoughts and emotions regarding an unplanned pregnancy and subsequent abortion. You may not be able to fully identify the loss that was incurred nor come to peace with God, yourself, and others. When this inability to process the abortion sets in, you may find yourself dealing with symptoms such as...

> *By affliction, the Lord separates the sin that He hates from the soul that He loves.*
>
> Rev. William Secker

- unresolved guilt regarding the abortion
- a heightened state of anxiety or apprehension
- denying the abortion happened or was wrong
- numbing through suppressed feelings, substance abuse, etc.
- suicidal thoughts or tendencies
- re-experiencing the abortion either through flashbacks or nightmares
- wanting to become pregnant again (replacement child)
- anxiety about childbearing issues, thinking God is going to punish you
- lack of bonding process with current children
- mourning the anniversary of the abortion or the due date

With those who have been affected by a friend or loved one's abortion, there are symptoms that stem from what is called "survivor's guilt." What we have seen the most in those who come to us for help are...

- Guilt for being allowed to live
- Lifelong struggles and questions about their existence
- Depression
- Feeling a responsibility to help their parents get better if they see them struggling to deal with the abortion

- Feeling disconnected from the family

There is no reason you should continue to carry these symptoms any further through your life. Let me ask you a question: Would you go to your doctor if you had a sickness you couldn't shake after a month? You would, wouldn't you? If you didn't, what do you think would happen to you? Your body? Your mind? Your job? Your relationships? Do you think they would suffer any? The wound from abortion is the same way.

Abortion leaves a gaping hole in your life and your heart, and it is a loss that is never grieved. As a loved one, you may feel a deep sense of injury knowing you are missing a key person from your life who was supposed to be there and affect your life in some way. I had a friend explain it to me this way:

"Abortion is like a gunshot wound to the leg. What do you think would happen if you were to be shot in the leg and never told anyone but just tried to deal with it on your own? You would go home, stop the bleeding, and put bandages on it as best you knew how. You would have to rethink your wardrobe because you would only be able to wear pants to cover up the wound so no one could find out.

Eventually, you would probably start to walk a little hunched over and with a limp because you had to deal with so much pain. The wound would subsequently get infected, seep into your bloodstream, and soon affect every limb of your body. The only way to get the wound healed at this point would be to take off all the layers of bandages, expose it to the light, scrape all the infection out, and let it breathe. This would take some time to heal and be extremely painful, but getting rid of the pain would be well worth it."

**Did you see yourself in any of that explanation?**
_____
_____

**Have you felt not right for a long time?**
_____
_____

**Have you tried to deal with the pain from the abortion alone?**
_____
_____
_____

**Have you put layers of protection around yourself, so no one can get to you and find out about any part you may have played in the abortion? If yes, how?**
_____
_____
_____

**Do you feel as if you are carrying a heavy burden for your loved one?**
_____
_____
_____

**Has this burden affected other areas of your life? If so, how?**
_____
_____

**Are you ready to expose your wound to the light so it can be healed?**

_____
_____
_____

Now, let's break this down and be a little more specific. You have different emotions that are affected by the trauma of abortion. Let's deal with these different emotions individually.

## The Emotion of Guilt

Everyone knows what guilt is, and everyone has experienced it. Guilt is when you know you've done something wrong, and you beat yourself up afterward. That is my own definition. *Webster's* says it is the fact of being responsible for the commission of an offense. So, the fact is, your friend or family member had an abortion. You may have helped encourage this abortion or tried desperately to keep them from it, but you still carry guilt for knowing a life you were connected to was lost.

I know every situation is different. You might not have known about the abortion until years later. Or you might have been right there through the whole thing. Whatever the situation, you must get to the root of any guilt you carry and allow God to remove it from your life.

Usually, there are three ways people deal with guilt. The first is by drowning it. Have you tried to drown your guilt with drugs, alcohol, eating, sex, or _____?

**Write out your method of drowning your guilt:**

_____
_____
_____
_____
_____
_____

> *It was very, very hard for me to believe, after all I had done, even after I abandoned God, He still, no matter how long it took me, forgave me.*
>
> *"Monica"*
> *in SaveOne class*

The second way people usually deal with guilt is by denying it. Our society has become more and more about manipulating or compromising our ethics to fit our situation. The lines for right and wrong have been blurred. We are now taught that guilt is an ancient concept, a rationalization that allows us to deny our choices are wrong. We find ourselves justifying abortion instead of realizing it is sin, and a line that should not have been crossed.

**How have you justified the abortion in the past?**

_____
_____
_____

**How have you denied the choice was wrong?**

_____
_____
_____

The third way people usually deal with guilt is by deflecting it. The choice for the abortion was ultimately your friend or loved one's choice to make. There are two ways you might be deflecting. Answer these questions...

**If you had nothing to do with the abortion decision, are you using knowledge of the abortion in any way to push guilt upon your loved one? If so, how?**

_____
_____

**If you had something to do with the abortion decision, are you deflecting guilt so as not to face your part in this decision? If so, how?**

_____
_____

**How long do you believe you or your loved one should feel guilty? Three months? Three years? A lifetime?**

_____
_____

**Name something from your past over which you felt guilt but don't anymore:**

_____
_____

**What made the guilt go away?**

_____
_____
_____

**Are there things you are doing to remind yourself or your loved one to feel guilty? If so, what are they?**

_____
_____
_____
_____

One thing I always did was put a star on my calendar on March 29 every year. That was the day I had my abortion. I felt as if I should kick myself for two weeks before and two weeks after. I would just be a wreck during that time. March 29 is now my youngest son's birthday. God truly wiped away my guilt.

Let's look to see what God tells us about guilt. Read **2 Samuel 11**. This is the story of David and the acts he committed.

**After reading this story, write below your thoughts toward David and what he did:**

_____
_____
_____
_____

Now **read Psalm 38:3-8**. David writes this passage after he has realized what he has done and how he grieved God.

**Does this describe the guilt you feel?**

_____
_____

**Do you believe David should have felt guilty? If so, for how long?**

_____
_____
_____
_____
_____
_____

**Read Acts 13:22.** God described David as "a man after my own heart, which shall fulfill all my will." God knew at this point the decisions, good and bad, that David would make.

> *There is no forgiveness from God unless you freely forgive your brother from your heart. And I wonder if we have been too narrow in thinking that "brother" only applies to someone else. What if YOU are the brother or sister who needs to be forgiven, and you need to forgive yourself?*
>
> *David Seamands*
> *Healing for Damaged Emotions*

**Now let's read Psalm 30. How does this describe David now?**

_____
_____

**Do you believe it is all right for David to feel this way after what he did? Why or why not?**

_____
_____

**Do you believe God can turn your mourning into dancing? Why or why not?**

_____
_____

You can't drown, deny, or deflect the guilt of an abortion. You must dissolve it through Christ Jesus.

**What did this section teach you about guilt?**

___

___

___

**What steps can you take this week to allow God to start dissolving your guilt?**

___

___

___

## The Emotion of Anger

Anger is an odd emotion. It's okay that we get angry, but God instructs us not to sin while we're angry **(Psalm 4:4)**. I believe He tells us that for our own protection. We do crazy things in our anger that we regret later. When anger is allowed to fester, it turns to rage.

**Explain one time in the past few weeks when you got angry:**

___

___

___

**What was your response?**

_____
_____
_____
_____
_____

> *Anger is an acid that can do more harm to the vessel in which it is stored than to anything on which it is poured.*
>
> *The Baptist Beacon*

**Was it the correct response?**

_____
_____
_____

**If no, what could you have done differently?**

_____
_____
_____

**Is your anger controlled? Or does your anger sometimes get out of control?**

_____
_____
_____
_____

**Do you get angry over stupid things? If so, give an example.**

_____
_____
_____
_____
_____

> *"What is righteous indignation?"* One child asked another.
>
> *"I don't know, but I think it means to get real mad and not cuss."*

After an abortion, some men and women will have angry outbursts and not understand where those outbursts come from. This comes from having anger that has been forced underneath the surface. It starts boiling underneath that surface, and it all comes gushing out at one little opening like an erupting volcano.

One way my anger was out of control was when I would be driving. It was like everyone around me had to watch out for me. If they didn't, that was it. I would yell and scream and keep my thumb on the horn at all times, just waiting to tell someone what I thought of him or her. I have been known to swerve at people to scare them after they cut me off or were going too slow for my taste. I know you think I must have been a tyrant. Actually, I was. When I see someone acting like that now, I just laugh and let that person go in front of me, or I wave to them and smile.

**What area of your life has a lot of anger in it?**

_____
_____
_____
_____

**What good does this anger do you?**

_____
_____
_____
_____

**Read Proverbs 25:28. What does this verse tell you about controlling your anger?**

_____
_____
_____
_____
_____

**Read Proverbs 15:1 and Proverbs 16:32. What do these two verses tell you about anger?**

_____
_____
_____
_____

> *I used to count to ten when becoming angry. But one day I thought of the first ten words of the Lord's Prayer.*
>
> *Now instead of counting to ten, I slowly say "Our Father, which are in Heaven, hallowed be thy name."*
>
> *Mrs. Fulton Oursler, whose husband wrote the classic book, The Greatest Story Ever Told*

**To accomplish being slow to anger and to acquire the ability to speak soft words, what trait would you have to master?**

_____
_____
_____

**Do you believe you can master self-control on your own? Why or why not?**

_____
_____
_____
_____

If self-control doesn't come easy for you when it comes to anger, God is there to help you refine that quality. You don't have to master it on your own. In fact, it's much easier when you allow God to work through you.

**What did this section teach you about anger?**

_____
_____
_____
_____

**What steps can you take this week to begin allowing God to work through you in the area of anger?**

_____
_____
_____
_____

Following are additional verses to study regarding anger. After reading these verses, turn to the journal pages at the end of this chapter. Write your thoughts about anger and what you have learned in this section about anger:

- **Psalm 37:8**
- **Proverbs 19:19**
- **Proverbs 14:17**
- **Hebrews 12:15**
- **Proverbs 17:27**
- **Ephesians 4:26**

## The Emotion of Sorrow

Sorrow: Mental suffering or pain caused by injury, loss, or despair. That's the definition *Webster's* gives us. Is this the way you feel when you think about the abortion? You're not alone. Abortion is a loss. Many people do not understand that this choice brings about a death, but no one is ever allowed to grieve this death. Grieving is a process you have to endure when you experience a loss. When you don't go through the grieving process, you stop growing in that area of your life, and you learn to just "manage" this unresolved grief. Until you allow yourself to grieve the loss of this child, you will always just be "managing" this sorrow instead of working through it and getting rid of it.

**Draw a picture of a person full of sorrow:**

**Read Psalm 6:6. Is this how you feel inside?**

_____
_____
_____
_____
_____

**Have you learned to manage your sorrow so well that you believe there is none?**

_____
_____
_____
_____
_____

> *Who doesn't make mistakes?! But the greatest error of all is to let any mistake destroy your faith in yourself.*
>
> *The only sensible course is to study and analyze why you made that mistake. Learn all you can from it, then forget it and go ahead. Figure on doing better next time.*
>
> *Norman Vincent Peale*

**Read Psalm 34:18.** Take a moment, put down this book, and talk to God. Concentrate solely on Him. Turn off any television, radio, or anything else that might distract you. Get alone and talk to God. Ask Him to reveal to you your hidden sorrow and which areas of your life have been affected. When you ask, He will answer. Don't discount what He tells you. Take as much time as you need.

**What areas of your life have been affected by sorrow?**

_____
_____
_____
_____

**Read John 11:1–44.** The people who were present after Lazarus died were full of sorrow. They had experienced the loss of Lazarus. They had no hope. With their human eyes, they saw Lazarus was dead and believed that was the end. But was it? When Jesus gets involved, things change.

> *When I first started the class I had no intention of "unveiling" my true self, or emotions.*
>
> *Somehow, without me even being aware of it, my shell was cracked and eventually removed.*
>
> *"Julie"*
> *in SaveOne class*

When you look at your situation with human eyes, you have no hope. You can't turn back the clock and change the choice that was made. You can't bring your loved one's child back and make everything all right. But is that the end of the story? No. Jesus can turn your sorrow into gladness and your mourning into dancing. I don't know how, but I know He can; I've experienced it firsthand. I lived for seven years with the horrific memory of abortion. When I allowed Jesus to work in my life and I allowed myself to receive His work, things changed.

The only way I can describe it is to say it was a supernatural transformation. I went from hating myself to loving Christ, and I went from contemplating suicide on a regular basis to enjoying life again. I went from thinking of my dead child to picturing her in Heaven, alive and well. I went from my secret shame to telling others so they could experience the same transformation.

This didn't happen to me because I'm more special than others. This happened because Jesus loves me in a way that no one else ever can. He loves you that same way. He wanted to wipe away my sorrow and tears. Just like Jesus, who in a moment's notice raised Lazarus from the dead, He wiped away their sorrow. He can wipe away yours, too.

Spend the next few moments talking to Jesus. Pour out your sorrow; tell Him how it has affected you. Tell Him you're ready to receive all He has for you. Be honest with Him and allow Him to work in your life. Then be very still and listen. He's there.

**Read Isaiah 51:3.** The comfort He is giving to Zion is the same promise He is telling you today.

**Write your scripture memory verse for the week:**
_____
_____
_____

**What did this section teach you about sorrow?**
_____
_____
_____

**What steps can you take this week to allow God to rid you of your sorrow?**
_____
_____
_____

*I took the Save One class because of a decision my daughter made over 18 years ago, a decision in which I was not consulted, a decision that took from me a child I will never meet on this earthly plain. This child had no name, no identity, and no future, and I was robbed of being a grandparent.*

*My daughter is haunted by her decision and lives in shame and regret. Through this class, I was able to forgive my daughter for her decision and begin to see some of what she was going through from her perspective. I quit blaming my daughter and myself. God gave me a physical and spiritual peace about her choice and the comfort of knowing that I will meet my granddaughter when I get to Heaven.*

*My granddaughter is no longer nameless, and I no longer live under shame and regret. I have such freedom from taking the class and highly recommend it to anyone who has gone through the pain of abortion, whether it was personally or through someone you are related to or even just know as a friend.*

*Letter from "Bettie" about her aborted granddaughter*

# JOURNAL PAGE

# CHAPTER 4
*Dealing With Stray Emotions: Part II*

Verse to memorize this week:
*Fear not; you will no longer live in shame. The shame of your youth and the sorrows of widowhood will be remembered no more.*

**Isaiah 54:4 NLT**

## The Emotion of Shame

Many people confuse guilt and shame, thinking they are the same emotion. They're not. Guilt says, "I made a mistake." Shame says, "I am a mistake." Shame goes to the core of your personhood. It is an internal feeling of you. This comes from your perception of who you think you should be, compared to who you believe you really are. The bigger the difference, the deeper the shame. All of this comes from your belief system: who you believe you are; the thoughts you believe about yourself; what you believe others are thinking of you. It's that belief system that has to be changed.

**Look up Romans 12:2. Write this verse below:**

_____

_____

_____

Renewing your mind is a simple thing, but it's a lifelong journey. Part of renewing your mind is realizing where these wrongful thoughts come from. Lewis Smedes says it best, "All unhealthy shame is rooted in deceit." Sure, you had a close friend or relative who had an abortion. But you have to realize that living in shame for the rest of your life isn't going to make it right, nor will it improve your life in any way.

We must not carry shame for another person's choices, even if we had a hand in that choice. I heard a pastor say one time, "When you live your life in shame, you are living beneath your destiny, destroying your sense of value. You must renew your mind, and then you begin to think differently about your problems." Renewing your mind doesn't happen overnight. It comes from a consistent study and meditation on God's Word.

Getting this word into your mind will release the bondage of shame from your life, tearing the root of deceit out of you that Satan has had there way too long.

**What are some of the things Satan has made you believe about yourself?**

_____

_____

_____

_____

> *We can no longer allow our minds to stay fixed on the past. We must reframe our expectations and walk forward in full confidence that He who has started a good work in us will finish it! (Philippians 1:6)*
>
> *Excerpt from "Finding You" by Sheila Harper*

Do the following shame statements sound familiar in any way?

- "If you knew me, you wouldn't love me."
- "I'm worthless."
- "There's no hope for me."
- "I've made too many mistakes."
- "I don't deserve to be forgiven."

**Add your own to the list. Write down three of your shame statements:**

1. _____
2. _____
3. _____

**Read Mark 10:27. What does this verse mean to you?**

_____

_____

**Do you believe it is possible for God to change your thought process?**
_____
_____
_____
_____
_____
_____

> *You can't take your failures and let them determine who you are. Identity isn't based on failure, but on Jesus Christ.*
>
> *Maury Davis*

**How will God achieve this?**
_____
_____
_____
_____

**Read II Corinthians 10:4–5. What is your part in this process?**
_____
_____
_____
_____

**How will you bring thoughts captive to the obedience of Christ?**
_____
_____
_____
_____

When you close a door to Satan, he eventually leaves you alone in that area because you are not vulnerable there anymore.

While going through this study, you will get into the habit of looking up scriptures, memorizing scriptures, and studying God's Word. I challenge you not to let this be the end of your study. The Bible holds the answers to all of life's questions, and it is as relevant in today's world as it was thousands of years ago when it was written. Many studies are available, just like this one, that go into other areas of your life. One that I've done is called *The Mind of Christ*, by Hunt and King. Another is *Experiencing God*, by Blackaby and King. A must-have is *The Battlefield of the Mind*, by Joyce Meyer.

> *Shame: painful feelings when there is a difference between who I think I should be and who I really am.*
>
> *Taken from the Hope Clinic training manual*

Just pick a study after you're through with this one and do it. Then pick another and do it. You're not in a hurry; you just want to remain consistent. If you continue, one day, you will run across this book and remember this time. You will flip open the pages, read your answers, and be shocked that you ever felt the way you do. You will see in vivid detail what God truly can do when you open yourself to Him and allow Him to change your thought process by renewing your mind. We will study more about renewing your mind in Chapter 8.

**What did this section teach you about shame?**

_____

_____

_____

**What steps can you take this week to start thinking differently about yourself or the area in which you harbor shame?**

> *All unhealthy shame is rooted in deceit.*
>
> Lewis Smedes

## The Emotion of Depression

**Read Psalm 6:2. If you battle with depression, is this how you feel sometimes?**

**Now read Psalm 34:18. Where is God when you are depressed?**

**Look up Proverbs 17:22.** Satan wants more than anything else to keep your spirit broken through depression. This verse says it "dries up your bones." You could reword that to say it dries up your entire life.

**Describe your depression below. Be specific.** What do you do when you're depressed? Do you stay in the house with the blinds closed? Do you drink alcohol? Do you stay in bed and remain inactive? Do you overeat? Do you become irritable and crabby? Do you want to stay away from people?

> *Living beneath your destiny destroys your sense of value.*
>
> *Maury Davis*

_____
_____
_____
_____

**Is this response a cure for depression or an intensifier for depression?**

_____
_____
_____
_____

**Draw your idea of what a depressed face looks like:**

**List below at least ten activities that are cures for depression:**

1. _____
2. _____
3. _____
4. _____
5. _____
6. _____
7. _____
8. _____
9. _____
10. _____

**Read Psalm 61:1-2.** This metaphor reminds us it doesn't matter where we are; there is always a higher place to go if we trust and rely on God. When your heart is overwhelmed, cry out to God and ask Him to lead you to the higher rock.

*Smooth seas do not make skillful sailors.*

*African proverb*

**Read Lamentations 3:22-23. Does God ever run out of mercy or compassion for you?**

_____
_____
_____

**Read Isaiah 40:31 and write it below:**

_____
_____

**What does this verse say He will do for you when you are depressed and lean on, trust in, and wait on God?**

_____

_____

_____

_____

_____

_____

> *Long-term depression over my abortion robs me of the ability to live a healthy, productive life. Depression consumes all of my energy. I can learn not to surrender to crippling depression.*
>
> *Luci Freed and Penny Salazar*
> *A Season to Heal*

**After reading all this scripture on depression, do you believe you will ever feel as though you are alone when you get depressed?**

_____

_____

_____

**Read Psalm 46:1 and Isaiah 40:29. What is God telling you in both scriptures?**

_____

_____

_____

**What did this section teach you about depression?**

_____

_____

_____

**What steps will you take this week to cure your depression?**

_____
_____
_____
_____

**Write your memory verse for the week:**

_____
_____
_____
_____

## The Emotion of...

**Write the name of any stray emotion that was not covered that you believe stems from the abortion:**

_____
_____
_____
_____
_____
_____

**Read Psalm 34:19. Do you believe God can deliver you? Why or why not?**

_____

_____

_____

_____

_____

> *With the goodness of God to desire our highest welfare, the wisdom of God to plan it, and the power of God to achieve it, what do we lack?*
>
> *A.W. Tozer*

**Look up at least three scriptures that pertain to this emotion, either through your Bible's concordance or a Bible website search. Write the scripture references below:**

_____

_____

_____

**Is there at least one of these verses that you can relate to? If so, which one?**

_____

_____

_____

**Write it below:**

_____

_____

_____

_____

**Why do you relate to this one?**

_____

_____

_____

_____

> *Connected with Him in His love, I am more than a conqueror; without Him, I am nothing.*
>
> *Corrie Ten Boom*

**Is there at least one verse that advises how to deal with this emotion? If so, which one?**

_____

_____

_____

**How?**

_____

_____

_____

**What did this section teach you about this emotion?**

_____

_____

_____

**What steps can you take this week to get this emotion under control?**

_____

_____

_____

Using what you have learned so far in this book, take the next few pages and write about this stray emotion. Take your time and write out your feelings, struggles, thoughts, and the cures for not letting this emotion get the best of you. Then write out anything else you have learned about your emotions through this chapter.

*My earliest memories are of the difficult times my family was having when I was a small child. I was four, and my parents were going through a nasty divorce. From a very young age, I knew my mother had chosen to have an abortion. It was told to me like she had no choice (my father was leaving us, and my mother had serious medical issues). I grew up thinking that if a doctor told you that you should have an abortion, then it was okay to have one.*

*The choices my parents made during that time permanently changed who I became. I have gone through some very difficult times emotionally in my life (deep depression and suicidal thoughts) because I never felt like I was able to grieve for the losses in my family properly. My family's way of dealing with emotional things is to deny they exist.*

*It wasn't until I began the SaveOne Bible study I realized that part of the loss of my family I was grieving was for my baby sister. I started this Bible study to try to help my mother, who has not moved forward with her life in many ways, but I quickly realized I needed to surrender my grief to Jesus as well.*

*Letter from "Sherry" about her aborted sibling*

## JOURNAL PAGE

# JOURNAL PAGE

# CHAPTER 5
*Forgiving Others*

Verse to memorize this week:
*And whenever you stand praying, if you have anything against anyone, forgive him, that your Father in Heaven may also forgive you your trespasses.*

**Mark 11:25-26**

For many of you, just reading the name of this chapter makes your heart rate increase. You have someone in your life who was actively involved in the abortion that you know you need to forgive. Others of you won't be able to think of anyone you haven't been able to forgive. Don't assume you can skip this chapter if you are one of those. This part is just as relevant to you as it is to the person whose heart is racing right now. A lack of forgiveness that stays on the back burner can poison your life if you let it.

> *The sin of unforgiveness is a cancer that destroys relationships, eats away at one's own psyche, and, worst of all, shuts us off from God's grace.*
>
> *Robertson McQuilkin*

We will go back and figure out exactly whom you may harbor any ill will toward, and we will resolve that in this chapter. Forgiving someone doesn't always happen overnight, but we will start the journey together.

Look back in Chapter 2 at the question that asked about your feelings toward any person who encouraged you to have an abortion. Also, look at the question that asked you to write down anyone toward whom you still felt anger or bitterness.

**What were your answers to these questions?**

_____
_____
_____
_____
_____
_____

**When you think of these people, do you experience any type of negative reaction? If so, what?**

_____

_____

_____

_____

_____

> *Doing an injury puts you below your enemy; revenging one makes you even with him; forgiving it sets you above him.*
>
> *Anonymous*

Let's look at an example of forgiveness. Read the following:

- **Genesis 37:3-4**
- **Genesis 37:23-28**
- **Genesis 39**
- **Genesis 41:14-15**
- **Genesis 41:37-41**
- **Genesis 42:6-8**
- **Genesis 45:1-15**

Can you believe all that Joseph endured? His brothers hated him, and he hadn't even done anything wrong. They were just jealous. He was thrown into a pit, left for dead, and then sold into slavery by his brothers. When he got to Egypt, he had to work as a slave. He was then framed for attempted rape and thrown into prison.

Even through all of this, he never stopped trusting God. That was the one constant in Joseph's life; trust in God. Because of this trust, God was with him, and he flourished everywhere he went. He was able to interpret Pharaoh's dream. Because of that, he was made the number two man in all of

Egypt. God took a horrible situation and turned it to Joseph's good because of his constant trust in God. Isn't it ironic that the brothers who hated Joseph so much had to turn to him in their time of need?

**Can you see how God worked in Joseph's life? Explain:**

_____
_____
_____
_____

**How did Joseph react to his brothers when they showed up for help?**

_____
_____
_____
_____

I admire Joseph for being able to still love and forgive his brothers. He had to endure all he did because of his brothers, yet he didn't hold a grudge against them. It would have been very easy for Joseph to withhold what his brothers needed out of spite. If he had done that instead, do you think God would have remained such a constant in Joseph's life?

**Read Luke 6:37 and write it below:**

_____
_____
_____
_____

I know forgiving others is a very hard thing to do, and it is especially hard to forgive if the other person shows no remorse. Look back at your verse to memorize this week. What does it say about the other person not being sorry for what they did? It doesn't say anything about the conditions you put on your forgiveness. The scripture simply says to forgive others so that you can be forgiven.

> *The New Testament tells me I can't take forgiveness myself and withhold it from others.*
>
> *Jerry Jenkins*

**Read 2 Thessalonians 1:6–7. In verse 6, what does it state God will do for you?**

_____

_____

_____

_____

**Read Romans 12:17–21. What does Christ tell us to do to our enemies?**

_____

_____

_____

_____

**Read Matthew 26:57–66. Why do you think Jesus didn't take up for Himself?**

_____

_____

_____

_____

**Read 1 Peter 2:21-23.** Jesus had perfect confidence in His Father, knowing He would judge his enemies justly.

**Let's look at another example of forgiveness. Read Acts 7:59-60. What was happening to Stephen?**

_____
_____
_____
_____

**Does it say the people who were stoning him were sorry?**

_____
_____

**How did Stephen react?**

_____
_____
_____
_____

**Which people associated with the abortion have you thought about forgiving if they showed remorse?**

_____
_____
_____
_____

**Who are you hurting by holding this grudge?**

_____

_____

_____

_____

_____

> *A Christian will find it cheaper to forgive than to resent. Forgiveness saves the expense of anger, the cost of hatred, the waste of spirits.*
>
> *Hannah More*

**Let's take a look at you for a moment. Write below a time when you did something wrong to someone, and they forgave you for it:**

_____

_____

_____

_____

**How did it make you feel?**

_____

_____

_____

_____

**Did it change the way you thought of that person? If so, how?**

_____

_____

_____

_____

**Why do you think God stresses so much in the Bible that we are to forgive others?**

_____
_____
_____
_____

**Read Luke 23:34.** Jesus forgave these men even though He knew they were about to kill Him. This is the ultimate example of forgiveness for us. Jesus paved the way for us to follow.

**Read Matthew 5:43-46. What are the four things Verse 44 instructs us to do?**

1. _____
2. _____
3. _____
4. _____

**Does it say anywhere in that passage to seek revenge on the people who have hurt you?**

_____

**Write Matthew 5:43-44:**

_____
_____
_____
_____

These scriptures go totally against our human nature. But God put them in the Bible for a reason. John Bevere (an exceptional author and speaker—I suggest reading any of his books) said it best when, in talking about these very verses, he said, "When we do this, our hearts are healed and cannot become critical or jaded."

Make a list of every person involved in the abortion to whom you still harbor ill feelings. Think back to the decision-making and all the way up through to the present day. Write the names of everyone. It could be the father, your sister, a mother-in-law, the doctor who performed the abortion, society for making abortion legal, or the family member or friend who chose abortion.

**Take your time and write this list below. If you run out of lines, keep writing somewhere until you get every name down on paper:**

_____
_____
_____
_____
_____
_____

> *It's the only solution I have found to retaliation and revenge, the only way I've been able to get past blame and resentment, the only antidote for secret, smoldering feelings of rage from the pain of my past. Forgiveness.*
>
> *Not until I fully forgave my offenders, one by one, name by name, offense by offense, did I gain the mastery over those tendencies within me to get back or to get even. I'm suggesting you will discover the same is true for you.*
>
> *Charles Swindoll*
> *Esther*

Take each of these names and say a prayer to God. Individually, ask God to help you forgive them. Be specific; ask Him to help you take your thoughts captive when you think of each person in a negative way. Ask Him to help you love them and soften your heart toward them. Then pray for something positive to happen in their life. Take this prayer very seriously because it can change your life if you believe what you are praying can and will happen.

Let's pray again. Put down this book and say a heartfelt prayer to God. Ask His forgiveness for holding this grudge toward these people for so long.

Now that you have asked forgiveness for all these things, that doesn't mean you won't have feelings and thoughts come up again toward those involved. If and when that happens, don't tell yourself you failed or that it didn't really work. Instead, remember this time and your prayer. God heard you and will bring your prayer to fruition if you continue to guard your heart and keep bad thoughts of these people away.

**Write Philippians 4:6-8:**

_____
_____
_____

**What do these verses tell us to think about?**

_____
_____
_____

These verses are in the Bible because God knew we would have bad thoughts come into our minds, and he is instructing us here on what to think about, so we can keep the ill will and the bitterness from creeping back into our lives.

I remember reading a certain story about forgiveness regarding a man named Rev. Walter H. Everett. He answered the phone one night only to hear the words no parent is ever ready to hear: **"Scott was murdered last night."** Walter's anger toward his son's killer raged, growing even worse when a plea bargain resulted in a reduced sentence for the attacker. His rage affected his entire life. He wondered how he would ever let go of the anger and forgive.

> *Real forgiveness means looking steadily at the sin, the sin that is leftover without any excuse, after all allowances have been made, and seeing it in all its horror, dirt, meanness, and malice, and nevertheless being wholly reconciled to the man who has done it.*
>
> C.S. Lewis

"The answer came the first time I saw Mike, almost a year after Scott's death. Mike stood in court before his sentencing and said he was truly sorry for his actions. Three-and-a-half weeks later, on the first anniversary of Scott's death, I wrote to Mike. I told him about my anger and asked some pointed questions. Then I wrote, 'Having said all that, I want to thank you for what you said in court, and as hard as these words are for me to write, I forgive you.' I wrote of God's love in Christ and invited Mike to write to me if he wished.

Three weeks later, his letter arrived. He said that when he read my letter, he couldn't believe it. No one had ever said to him, *'I forgive you.'* That night he had knelt beside his bunk and prayed for and received the forgiveness of Jesus Christ. Additional correspondence led to regular visits during which we often spoke of Mike's (and my) growing relationship with Christ. Later I spoke on Mike's behalf before a parole board, and he was given an early release. In November 1994, I was the officiating minister at his wedding."

When asked about his early release, Mike says, "It felt good, but I was already out of prison. God had set me free when I asked for his forgiveness."

Can I truly forgive? I had wondered if it were possible. But I've discovered the meaning of the Apostle Paul's words: "For freedom, Christ has set us free."

**What did this section teach you about forgiving others?**
_____
_____

**What steps can you take this week to further heal these relationships?**
_____
_____

**Write your memory verse for the week:**
_____
_____

Use one of the journal pages that follow to write what you would like to say to the people you have forgiven through this chapter.

*"Abortion survivors must be able to see that parental love is real. When they see it in people, they then can understand that God, as our Father, can be loving toward them. They need to understand that they are welcome in God's family and that when they have God's Spirit within them, He gives purpose, joy, and meaning to their lives. Salvation through Jesus Christ is both the cause and effect in the healing process."*

*Dr. Phillip Ney, who has completed extensive research on the effects of abortion on siblings.*

## JOURNAL PAGE

## JOURNAL PAGE

# CHAPTER 6
*God's Grace*

Verse to memorize this week:
"Let us, therefore, come boldly to the throne of grace, that we may obtain mercy and find grace to help in time of need."

**Hebrews 4:16**

**What is your definition of grace?**

_____
_____
_____

For years I didn't really have a definition of grace. Grace was one of those churchy words I grew up hearing all the time and singing about, but I never took the time to really think about what grace meant. One day I was asked to give a talk at a spiritual retreat. The topic was grace. As I studied for my talk, the understanding of God's grace really became clear to me.

**Grace means "undeserved love and favor." Write that in the space provided:**

_____

How often have we withheld something from someone, or something was withheld from us because we didn't "deserve" it? God doesn't think that way. He created us and has an unending supply of undeserved love and favor with your name on it.

**Write your name in the blank:**

_____ has an unending supply of love and favor.

**Read 1 Peter 2:9 and write it below:**

_____
_____

**Who does this verse say you are?**

_____
_____

Let's look at some examples of God's grace and how far it extends. Remember back in Chapter 5, where we read a little bit about Stephen and how he forgave the people who were stoning him?

**Read Acts 7:58.** This mentions a man named Saul. Pay attention to him. Let's read a little bit more about who he was and what he was about.

> *Forgiveness is not forgetting, because I could never forget what I did. But forgiveness is knowing that is what Jesus died for.*
>
> *"Jessica"*
> *in SaveOne class*

**Read Acts 8:1, 3.** Saul had a murderous hatred for all Christians and gave the go-ahead to kill Stephen because Stephen was a Christian. Saul also led the persecution against the church, as written in verse one. Saul murdered and imprisoned innocent people simply because they believed in God.

**Read Acts 9:1-9.** This chapter starts out by telling us about Saul's receiving even more authority to imprison Christians. He is on his journey when the audible voice of Jesus Christ speaks to him. I believe that got his attention because he fell to the ground. Jesus asks Saul why he is persecuting Him. He asked this because attacking a child of God is a direct attack on Christ Himself. He then struck Saul blind for three days.

My opinion is that God had to do that to get Saul to slow down long enough to think about what was going on. Sometimes we get too busy with our lives. There are moments when we don't take the time to just simply sit and listen to what God has to tell us, even when we are working for Christ. This was a huge turning point in Saul's life. God wanted him to realize the seriousness of what was about to happen.

**Read Acts 9:20-22.** Saul did a complete turnaround, didn't he? He immediately started telling people that Jesus was Lord. God extended His grace to

Saul, who had committed murder, victimized the church, and imprisoned innocent believers.

**Remember the definition of grace? What is it?**

_____
_____

**Saul definitely received undeserved love and favor. What does this story tell you about God's grace?**

_____
_____
_____

John Bevere has another definition for grace: "God's empowering presence." Saul experienced God's presence. It is that presence in our lives that empowers us to do things we normally could not. Because of God's grace, Saul was truly forgiven and changed. He became one of the greatest witnesses for Christ in history.

**Read 2 Corinthians 9:8. Do you believe this same grace is for you and your loved one today? Why or why not?**

_____
_____
_____

**Read Joel 2:25, and write it below:**

_____
_____
_____

**What does this verse say God will do for you?**

_____
_____
_____

**Read Ephesians 2:8-9.** Saved doesn't just mean salvation. The term can mean anything Satan may throw at you; bondage, guilt, shame, regret, sin in anger, and depression. Our works cannot save us from these things, but laying these things down allows Jesus Christ to save us from them by His grace... His undeserved love and favor.

**Read Isaiah 55:7. What are the three actions we have to take?**

1. _____
2. _____
3. _____

**After these three actions, what does that verse say God will then do?**

_____
_____
_____

**Have you ever asked God to forgive you for your involvement in the abortion? Or have you asked God to forgive you for withholding grace toward your friend or loved one because of the abortion?**

_____
_____
_____

**Read Matthew 7:7-11. What do these verses tell you about asking something of God?**

_____

_____

_____

_____

If you have never asked God to forgive you for any involvement you had in the abortion or for withholding grace, I would like for you to take a moment, put down this book, and talk to God as you would a friend. Confess your involvement to Him **(Psalm 32:5)**, talk to Him about it, and ask Him to forgive you. Take as long as you need. This is between you and God. If you were in no way involved in your friend or family member's abortion, then take this time to pray for your loved one.

> *My daughter is haunted by her decision and lives in shame and regret. Through this class I was able to forgive my daughter for her decision and to begin to see from her perspective some of what she was going through for her decision.*
>
> *I quit blaming myself and my daughter. God gave me a physical and spiritual peace about the choice she made, and that I will meet my grand-daughter when I get to heaven.*
>
> *"Linda"*
> *in SaveOne class*

**After doing this, write below how this exercise made you feel and what you gained from it:**

_____

_____

_____

**Read Isaiah 38:17 and Psalm 103:12. What does God do with our sins once we have asked for forgiveness?**

_____

Did you know God cannot tell a lie? He is perfect and without sin. If His word states He will remove our sin from us as far as the east is from the west, then that is what He HAS to do.

**Write Isaiah 43:25:**

_____

_____

_____

_____

> *I was robbed of being a grand-parent. But the healing that came through this class is just overwhelming and needs to be experienced by anyone affected by this sin.*
>
> *"Steve"*
> *in SaveOne class*

**Through what you have learned in this chapter, write in your own words how God forgives you of your sin:**

_____

_____

_____

You may not instantly "feel" forgiven. Don't worry about that. Don't even think about it. What you have to know for sure is that your forgiveness is not based on your feelings. Think of how your feelings change from day to day. One day you might feel happy, the next day, you might feel irritated, and yet the next day, you might feel stressed. That doesn't change who you truly are just because you feel differently from day to day. So one could only suppose the same is true with your feelings of forgiveness. Believe in the scriptures you have studied over the past weeks. Know that you know that you have been forgiven.

**What did this section teach you about God's grace?**

_____
_____
_____

**What steps can you take this week to put this knowledge into practice?**

_____
_____
_____

**Write your memory verse for the week:**

_____
_____

Close this chapter by reading **Psalm 32.** In fact, read it three times. Get it in your mind and remember it always, so on those days you don't "feel" forgiven, you can turn to this chapter and remember God's grace.

*Maybe you were like me and thought abortion had not touched your family. I have come to realize that very few families have not been affected by abortion because it is such a secret. My eyes were opened to the truth.*

*I participated in a SaveOne study after my Mom shared her 40-plus-year secret. She had an abortion before becoming pregnant with me. In this one moment, my childhood made sense. I soon discovered, through the study, the effects an abortion has on a person. The enemy of her soul had stolen her motherhood.*

*I discovered the lie the enemy tells each one of the women is the same hopelessness. She didn't have a safe place to share her grief and carried such a heavy burden. Silence became her friend; shame a daily companion. There was sadness in the depths of her soul that could be seen in her eyes.*

*One of the chapters in the SaveOne book gave me insight into the depression, suicidal tendencies, and lack of bonding we experienced growing up. My mother loved me, but she was stricken with grief and shame to the point she could not express her love. I began to see my Mom through new eyes of love and compassion for all she had lost and the torment that came with it. My longing for her to receive forgiveness and restoration became my daily prayer. My sisters became real to me, and I knew deep in my heart that they also wanted this for our Mom. I'm happy to share that she has been REDEEMED and reunited with her girls. My Mom is a great woman of courage, and I love to honor her.*

*Letter from "Jeri" about her aborted siblings*

## JOURNAL PAGE

# CHAPTER 7
## *Can I Forgive Myself?*

Verse to memorize this week:
*For you shall know the truth, and the truth shall make you free. For if the Son makes you free, you shall be free indeed.*

**John 8:32, 36 NLT**

We've talked a lot about forgiveness throughout this book, but what we're about to discuss in this chapter is all about you. For now, don't think of anyone you wrote about in the previous chapters. I only want you to think about yourself all during this week.

> *To live is to forgive: even oneself.*
>
> *Anonymous*

David Seamands, the author of *Healing for Damaged Emotions*, writes, "There is no forgiveness from God unless you freely forgive your brother from your heart. And I wonder if we have been too narrow in thinking that "brother" only applies to someone else. What if YOU are the brother or sister who needs to be forgiven, and you need to forgive yourself?"

Let's review your progress. So far, you have developed a proper perspective of the loving, forgiving God He wants to be in your life. He is your source of courage! Through your asking, God has crushed that heavy wooden yoke of abortion grief you had been carrying around your neck for way too long. You made yourself remember details of the abortion experience to bring those memories out of the darkness and into the light. You realize stepping into the light is the only way to heal this wound. You finally can put a name—Post Abortion Syndrome—to your symptoms. You have dealt with your emotions of guilt, shame, sorrow, depression, and anger. You have learned of true forgiveness and pinpointed the people involved in the abortion you needed to forgive. Then as hard as it was, you forgave them. You have learned about God's undeserved love and favor and how far it extends. You have asked God to forgive you for your involvement in the abortion, and through this same grace, He has. Be proud of yourself for making such progress! Do you realize what you have accomplished over the past few weeks? Now we only have a little way to go before this time of healing is complete. Like I said at the beginning of the chapter, this week we're going to focus on you.

**Write Romans 8:37:**

_____
_____
_____

In my Bible, the explanation for this verse states this: to conquer completely without any real threat to personal life or health.

**Are you ready to conquer this thing once and for all?**

_____
_____
_____

**Read Romans 3:23. Who does this verse say has sinned?**

_____
_____
_____

A pastor once told me, "Your righteousness lives in your faith, not your feelings, not your circumstances. If you abide in Christ, you are always on steady ground." We must remember to believe in knowing we are forgiven and not go by our feelings or circumstances. Those things change constantly, but who Christ is and what He has done in our lives do not change.

**Read Philippians 4:6-7. What do these verses tell you your actions have to be?**

_____
_____
_____

**What do these verses tell us Christ will do?**

_____

_____

_____

I've written out of the New Living Translation, **Mark 11:24**. I like this version because it's plain and to the point: "Listen to me! You can pray for anything, and if you believe, you will have it."

Like I stated in a previous chapter, God cannot tell a lie. If it is written in the Bible, it is the absolute truth. God will not waver from His truth. If you are truly sick of carrying this burden around, then it's time to pray. I don't want you to start thinking you are not worthy to pray this prayer. NONE of us are worthy regardless of what our past holds; that's when God's grace and our faith are enacted. Pray this prayer with boldness and authority from God. He has brought you this far, and He's not about to leave you now. Let go of any bad thoughts you are having and prepare your mind to pray.

In a passage in **Luke 11:1**, one of Jesus's disciples asked Him to teach them how to pray. Jesus replied, "When you pray, say Our Father which art in Heaven, Hallowed be thy name. Thy kingdom come. Thy will be done in earth, as [it is] in Heaven. Give us this day our daily bread. And forgive us our debts, as we forgive our debtors. And lead us not into temptation but deliver us from evil. For thine is the kingdom, and the power, and the glory, forever. Amen."

Now, I realize this is a prayer you've heard before. You may have breezed through it because it was so familiar, but let's study it for a moment. You start out talking to your Father, and you tell Him that hallowed is His name. Hallowed is praise. You're telling God you want to set His name apart as being holy, respected, and honored. You're telling God you want His kingdom to come soon. You want His will to be done here where you are, just as it would be if you were in Heaven. You are asking God for your daily bread, which could be translated to mean your entire daily needs. He is teaching us right here to trust Him daily, and let tomorrow worry about itself. Then you asked His forgiveness for your sins (debts) because you are forgiving those who have sinned against you.

> *Change is both a challenge and a threat. It represents everything I hope for, and everything I fear.*
>
> Dale Hansenbourke

As you learned in previous chapters, these two go hand in hand. Then you have asked Him not to let you be led into temptation or do things you know you shouldn't but to take you away (deliver) from any evil. Evil isn't just the big ones, sex outside marriage, drugs, alcohol, etc. Evil can be wrong thoughts, unforgiveness, and the list goes on. Anything that doesn't line up with scripture can be considered evil if used in the wrong way. Then the prayer is again closed with praise.

One of the dear saints of God I had the privilege to know is Sister Alice Jane Blythe. She asked me to eat lunch with her. I was very honored. While at lunch, she told me of a family situation she was in one time, and how she allowed Satan to make her worry. She tossed and turned for nights, and she had a hard time concentrating on anything. Finally, God woke her up one night and told her to pray. He said, "Pray this way, Our Father which art in Heaven, hallowed be thy name, thy kingdom come, thy will be done on earth as it is in Heaven. Give us this day our daily bread. And forgive us our debts, as we forgive our debtors. But lead us not into temptation, but deliver us from evil. For thine is the kingdom, and the power, and the glory, forever. Amen." She told me that any time I pray, to hold up my prayer beside this perfect prayer, and I will always be okay.

After praying this prayer that night, she had total peace. Her worry went away. She enacted her faith, which is believing God's word is true no matter what your circumstances seem to be.

> *It's not whether you get knocked down, it's whether you get up again.*
>
> Vince Lombardi

**Can you do things that God cannot?**

___

**If God has let go of your sin, then how can you still hold on to it?**

___

Holding on to sin that is forgiven would be like a man being released from prison but refusing to go. What message are you sending Him when you hold on to your sin after God has let it go? You are, in essence, telling Him that sending His Son to die on the cross was not enough to forgive you of your sin. You are telling Him your sin is too great for His sacrifice to cover. You are trying to be mightier than God. Now I know that might seem a little harsh. I know you never consciously set out to tell God all these things. But not believing or putting into practice what His Word says is just continuing on the path God never intended for you. When you do this, you never allow yourself to live fully in the present because of the hold you keep on yourself from the past.

**How do you think this affects your daily life?**

**How do you think this affects your present relationships?**

> *God's love has taken off my chains, and given me these wings.*
>
> *Stephen Curtis Chapman*

_____

_____

_____

_____

_____

Are you ready to pray? I have written out a prayer below. Pray it out loud with the boldness and authority of someone ready to start a new life:

*Dear Heavenly Father,*
*I praise You and thank You, Lord! You have given me so much, and for that, I am so grateful.*

*I want to ask You right now, Lord, to hear my prayer. This is one of the most important prayers I have ever prayed in my life, and I don't want anything to stand in the way of You hearing it, so please wipe away any sin in my life. I want to be spotless before You. Lord, I want only Your will for my life. I know that You created me in Your image, and your image does not include all the baggage that came with my loved one's abortion. I am ready to lay this baggage down. I have been mentally and physically drained at times from carrying it around, and I know now that it is not Your will for my life.*

*Lord, I want my life to reflect Your will as it is in Heaven. I want to walk as closely to You here on this earth as I physically can. Lord, I will trust You daily. Please help me when I start to worry about the past or when I don't "feel" forgiven. Remind me to enact my faith. Let me have the peace of knowing it doesn't matter how I feel. My faith and Your word tell me I am forgiven. I have learned if You have forgiven me, I can no longer hold on to this pain. Deliver me from it forever,*

*Lord. I lay it down once and for all, never to pick it up again. The pain, shame, sorrow, and regret I have felt from the choice of abortion no longer have a hold on me. Thank You, Lord Jesus, for giving me the boldness and authority I needed to pray this prayer. I will forever love You and praise Your name!*

> *I am free.*
>
> *"Penny"*
> *in SaveOne class*

*In Jesus' name, I pray, Amen.*

**Read Isaiah 44:22.** *Webster's* defines the word redeemed as follows:

- To set free, rescue, or ransom.
- To save from a state of sinfulness and its consequences.

That's what you are - redeemed! You have been set free, and you have been Rescued. You have been saved from a state of sinfulness **AND** its consequences! You no longer have to carry around the hurt, pain, guilt, or baggage of your friend or family member's abortion.

**What did this section teach you about forgiveness?**

_____

_____

_____

**What steps can you take this week to put this knowledge into practice?**

_____

_____

_____

**Read Psalm 30 to close out this chapter. Write your memory verse for the week.**

_____

_____

_____

Below is a letter from my sister Kim used with her permission. These are hard words for me to read but necessary words to speak. Families hurt after abortion).

*To actually feel when I think of her is almost too much. I feel short of breath as I imagine how alike she and my own daughter would probably have been. And as my tears start to flow, I wonder if she would have been tall like her mother or if she maybe would have looked like me since my daughter looks so much like my sister.*

*The sadness I feel in knowing what we lost that day, what my little sister lost that day, makes my heart hurt! How can someone actually reason that out and then convince others to kill their very own child and that it's okay??*

*An innocent, helpless baby, and I couldn't protect her? Oh, how I want to tell her how sorry I am that I wasn't there for her! I didn't get to meet her! I didn't even know about her until it was too late! This makes me so angry and sad at the same time!*

*And even now, as I read my thoughts, I realize no words can do justice to the feelings, the absolute heartbreak and anger of an Aunt knowing her only niece was murdered while still in her mother's womb and that someone thought that was okay...*

## JOURNAL PAGE

## JOURNAL PAGE

# CHAPTER 8

*Renewing Your Mind*

Verse to memorize this week:
*Don't copy the behavior and customs of this world, but let God transform you into a new person by changing the way you think. Then you will know what God wants you to do, and you will know how good and pleasing and perfect His will really is.*

**Romans 12:2 NLT**

When you renew your mind, you think differently about your problems. When you don't renew your mind, Satan has a playground to torment you. Satan will bombard you with wrong thinking as much as you will let him. I am here to tell you; you don't have to let him! Renewing your mind is simply training it to believe and think only the thoughts that line up with the Word of God.

> *The mind of man is the battleground on which every moral and spiritual battle is fought.*
>
> *J. Oswald Sanders*

Satan is a liar. **Read John 8:44.** Jesus tells us ". . . there is no truth in him." Let's look at some thoughts you might have or have had, and see if they line up with scripture. In the blank provided, **write S** if the thought is from Satan; **write G** if the thought lines up with the word of God:

_____ "I need to remind myself of my loss through abortion. That way, I will honor the memory of the child."

**Read Philippians 4:8.**

_____ "I am a horrible person. What kind of person would have any involvement with an abortion?"

**Read Colossians 3:10.**

_____ "It's okay to talk about the abortion because I'm forgiven for my involvement, or I have forgiven those involved."

**Read John 8:36.**

_____    "I don't deserve to be forgiven."

**Read Romans 3:23.**

_____    "I need to think about my loved one's child and one day seeing him/her. What a wonderful day that will be!"

**Read Philippians 4:8.**

**Read John 10:10.** Satan came to kill, steal, and destroy. He has stolen enough of your life away by keeping the abortion at the forefront of your mind. Read the second part of that verse again. Jesus came so you will have life and have it more abundantly. It is time to reclaim the years Satan has stolen from you by renewing your mind.

Decide right now that you will not allow him to steal any more time from your life. Speak to him and confess it out loud. He can't see your thoughts like Christ can, but He can certainly hear you.

**Do that now in your own words, and then write down what you said to Him.**

_____
_____
_____

**Write Philippians 4:8.**

_____
_____
_____
_____

These are the things we should be thinking about. When you have a thought that twists your mind, you can hold it up and ask yourself, Is this pure? Is this noble? Is this a good report? Is this a lovely thought? If it is not, then bring it into captivity.

> *Our defeat or victory begins with what we think, and if we guard our thoughts we shall not have much trouble anywhere else along the line.*
>
> *Vance Havner*

**Read 2 Corinthians 10:4-5. What is a stronghold?**

_____
_____
_____

**Where do our weapons come from, according to this scripture?**

_____
_____
_____

**What does this scripture mean when it says we are to cast down any high thing that exalts itself against the knowledge of God?**

_____
_____
_____

**What are we supposed to do with our thoughts?**

_____
_____
_____

**How do we bring our thoughts into captivity to the obedience of Christ?**

_____
_____
_____

When, not if, Satan throws these darts at you, reminding you of your past, you need to have a plan of action to conquer him. When you accomplish something grand, like what you are doing right now by allowing God to heal your past, Satan will do all he can to try to tell you it wasn't real. He will throw these darts at your most vulnerable areas.

**Read Matthew 9:17. How can you relate this verse to your mind?**

_____
_____
_____

You can't have a new life with an old way of thinking. Set a new standard for yourself and your future. You don't have to accept past defeats. You have the opportunity right now to break the negative cycle in your life. Get rid of the old wineskin and get ready for God to change your life.

Let me tell you a story of one girl who came to one of my SaveOne classes. I recognized her immediately as the lady I had seen pushing her son around the church in his wheelchair. The first night she couldn't speak; she was crying so hard. During introductions, she was able to get out her name, but that was it. The following week she came back and proceeded to tell us her story. She had had an abortion years before, and later, after marriage, she became pregnant again. She gave birth to a son who had cerebral palsy. From then on, she believed she could never tell anyone about her abortion.

She feared that everyone would look at her son in his wheelchair and believe that was God's condemnation of her life. When she said this in class, the realization of just how despicable Satan is became clear to me. If he will take the most innocent of creation, a disabled child, and use him against his own mother, he will stop at nothing.

> *You cannot stay where you are and go with God.*
>
> *Blackaby and King*
> *Experiencing God*

My friend, Donna, has come so far since that night. She finished the class and drove out the lie Satan had made her believe for so long. She now teaches our SaveOne classes and can talk about her past without any condemnation.

The key is she renewed her mind. She allowed God to make her thinking new. She held up that lie from Satan against the word of God and realized it simply was not true. Satan will finally leave you alone when you become stronger; he realizes this is no longer a vulnerable area for you.

I once heard a pastor say, "Confessing the word of God by faith corrects my mental picture." When you think wrong thoughts, have a counterthought ready. Look back on those statements at the beginning of this chapter. You may also want to look at the shame statements from Chapter 4. What is a counter thought that lines up with the Word of God for each of the statements that are from Satan? Write them in the following blanks:

**Example:**
Shame statement: "I'm worthless."
Positive confession: "I am created in the image of God. Therefore, I have great worth in the eyes of God!"

_____

_____

_____

_____

_____

_____

_____

Learn these statements, and then as Satan throws the darts, you will have a positive confession from the Word of God to fight them. State them out loud at each occurrence. That will be your confession, further correcting your mental picture. You might ask, "Sheila, how do you expect me to have a good mental picture after all I've been through?"

Maybe, by looking at my picture on the back of this book, you assume I've got it all together and that I've always had this great life. Let me tell you that hasn't always been the case. I've made many bad choices that resulted in horrific consequences, such as a past rape, my abortion, drug abuse, and alcohol abuse. Before that, I suffered some horrific consequences because of other bad decisions that had nothing to do with me, such as sexual, physical, and mental abuse as a child. I know often, but not always, abortion is just a furtherance of a pattern of abuse throughout a person's life. But I can tell you from experience your life doesn't have to continue on this path. Because of my good choices, I bring about good consequences, resulting in a positive life. You no longer have to be a victim. Turn your will toward God and allow him to work.

There is a line from an old song I love that goes, "Take my will and mold it in your pleasure." By allowing your past and whatever may be there to dictate your future, your thoughts then tie God's hands. You're not allowing Him to do great work in you. You need to let Him take your will and mold it as He pleases.

**Read Philippians 1:6.** God is trying to do a great work in you. But He will not go against your will. You have to renew your mind and stop allowing your past to make you think negatively. Negative thoughts create a negative person.

> *Every temptation comes to us via our thoughts.*
>
> Erwin Lutzer
> Those Sins That
> Won't Budge

**Read Proverbs 23:7.** What you think, you will be. If you think of yourself as a victim, then that is all you will ever be. You will never taste the sweet victory God has for you. Allow God to take your past and whatever may be in it and turn it into His mighty tool to help others.

**Read Psalm 119:93.** My Bible uses the word precepts in this verse, which means a particular course of action. In essence, this verse is saying, "to never forget God's course of action He gives you, because by this He has given you life."

**Where can you find God's course of action?**

_____

_____

_____

I hope your answer was the Bible. This is where you find all your answers. This is where the basis for renewing your mind will always come from. This is where you need to be to get God's word implanted deep inside you for future reference. Don't let this be the end of your study. You have developed the habit of studying, looking up scripture, and memorizing scripture over these past few weeks. Don't let this study be the end.

Continue on after you have finished this book. You will find the renewal process so much more pleasant than the alternative.

Seeds have been planted in your mind that need time to grow. Don't give up. Renewing your mind is a process. It's not something that is going to happen overnight and then "keep." Renewing your mind is a lifelong journey that is a marvelous journey.

> *You cannot have a positive life and a negative mind.*
>
> *Joyce Meyer*
> *Battlefield of the Mind*

**What did this section teach you about the renewal of your mind?**
___
___
___

**What steps can you take this week to put this knowledge into practice?**
___
___
___

**Write your memory verse for the week:**
___
___

*I thought driving my friend to the clinic was no big deal. In fact, I felt really good about myself for taking her because she seemed so desperate. No one else would agree to, so I felt like her knight in shining armor.*

*I walked in with her, and it felt really creepy. They took her back, and the longer I sat there, the more repulsed I felt. I finally couldn't stay inside any longer, and I went to the car and sat in the parking lot just so I could get out of there. I will never forget the smells and the sounds of that place. I will also never forget my friend's face when she walked out of there. I knew something really terrible had happened to her.*

*We never spoke of that day again, but my friend seemed more distant every week that passed. She never returned to school after that semester and I have no idea where she is now. I have carried the guilt of that day with me my entire life. I have never told my wife or anybody else, for that matter. My wife had a miscarriage not long after we married, and I always felt like it was my fault for being "an accessory to murder."*

*A knight in shining armor was the LAST thing I was. I know my friend probably hates me now for agreeing to participate in such an ugly, horrible day for her. I would give anything to go back to that day and be the one who stood up for what was right and maybe talk her out of it. There's not a day that goes by that I don't think about it.*

*"Tom" in SaveOne class*

## JOURNAL PAGE

# CHAPTER 9
## *Who Is This Child?*

Verse to memorize this week:
*Let us draw near with a true heart in full assurance of faith, having our hearts sprinkled from an evil conscience, and our bodies washed with pure water. Without wavering, let us hold tightly to the hope we say we have, for God can be trusted to keep his promise.*

**Hebrews 10:22-23 NLT**

This course you are taking is about life, reclaiming your own life as well as giving honor and distinction to the child who is missing from your life. Through the work you will do in this chapter, you will bestow the dignity and honor on the child he/she so deserves. When this child's soul was ushered into Heaven, he/she became part of a nameless, faceless sea of statistics. This is your opportunity to change all of that.

> *She became a real person to me. It was like, instead of nine months and delivering a baby, I spent twelve weeks working through the past and delivering a fifteen-year-old daughter.*
>
> *She is so real to me now.*
>
> *"Ann"*
> *in SaveOne class*

Have you ever allowed yourself to think about the child who was lost? Have you ever wondered if the child was a boy or girl? Have you ever wondered what he/she looks like? Don't be afraid to think these thoughts. I know there will be pain involved in finding the answers to these questions. But Christ is still here with you.

**Read Deuteronomy 31:6, 8. What two things will God <u>not</u> do?**

1. _____
2. _____

He was with you when you started this book, and He is still here now. He is intimately involved in every detail of your life. Please take a moment and say a prayer asking God to give you His peace and comfort that goes above and beyond our human comprehension **(Philippians 4:7)** as you work through this chapter.

One of the most common uncertainties you might have is whether this child was a boy or a girl. You might believe this is a question you will never know until you reach Heaven, but this is simply not true. You don't have to accept this uncertainty and remain in the dark. God knows the answer to your question. He will tell you if you ask. He has always known this child. **Jeremiah 1:5** says, "Before I formed you in the womb I knew you . . . " He is right there in Heaven with him or her. As hard as this might be, I want you to put down this book right now and take as long as you need. Talk to God; tell Him you have remained in the dark long enough. Tell Him you are ready to give this child life. Then ask Him to reveal to you the child's gender. (*Oftentimes, the mother or father will have a strong urging as to the gender of their child. If the lines of communication are open with the mother or father of this child, you might want to ask them if they believe their child was a male or female*).

**Finish this sentence: My loved one's child is a _____.**

**Do you believe this child is in Heaven? Why or why not?**

_____
_____
_____

**2 Corinthians 5:8** in the New Living Translation says, "Yes, we are fully confident, and we would rather be away from these bodies, for then we will be at home with the Lord."

To be absent from your body is to be present with the Lord. Your loved one's child never got to experience life here on this earth. Therefore he/she never had the opportunity to sin or develop any bad habits that would keep him/her out of Heaven. When the child's soul left his/her body, it was pure, blameless, and spotless before the Lord.

Now that you know if the child was a boy or girl, I want you to think for a moment about his/her physical characteristics. Would she be tall? Would he have curly hair? Would she be musical? Would he love baseball?

**Write in detail what you believe this child's appearance and personality would be:**

_____

_____

_____


**Are you starting to see your loved one's child? Can you picture him/her in Heaven? What do you think life is like for him/her in Heaven?**

_____

_____

_____


You now have an image of the child. You might have seen her running the bases. You might be picturing him riding a bike. Whatever your mind sees of the child, whether it's a tiny baby or a grown woman, this person in Heaven needs a name.

Naming the child will give you a great sense of identification with him/her. It will be one more step in giving this child life and recognizing him/her as a human being worthy of a name. This name is what plucks the child out of that sea of nameless, faceless statistics and makes him/her stand tall and proud. Again, take some time for uninterrupted prayer (*Again, if the lines of communication are open with the mother or father of this child about this subject, you might want to consult them through this process*).

**Name the child. Write name(s) below:**

_____

_____

_____

**Read Revelation 21:4. What four things does it say will be no more?**

1. _____

2. _____

3. _____

4. _____

**How can these four things be no more?**

_____

_____

_____

_____

**If you had an opportunity to talk with your loved one's child, what would you say?**

The following exercise (page 142) is simply an occasion for you to say the things you would like to say to this child but didn't get the chance.

This is not a literal exercise, actually speaking to the child in any way, but rather just an opportunity to get off your mind what you would like to say.

It's for your eyes only.

> At times, I imagine I see your face in the wind, in a beautiful sunset, or when I look into a rainbow. I see us walking hand in hand, with your beautiful blond curls about your face, and eyes as beautiful as the sky. When I come back to reality, I know that when I enter Heaven's gates, you will be there to meet me and we will walk hand in hand.
>
> *"Joni"*
> *excerpt from letter to child*

**Dear** _____,

There is one more thing I want you to do. Giving this child a place of honor within your home is another exercise in bestowing dignity. Creating a memorial will bring this child into his/her rightful place into your family or simply give honor as someone you lost. This doesn't have to be anything elaborate. My memorial to my daughter Meghan is simply a pink candle in a tulip candleholder. It sits in the middle of a table full of family photos. I don't have a picture of my daughter, but I can place the memorial for her alongside the pictures of the other people I love.

> *I know you have a home with God and He embraces you with his loving arms, I am eternally thankful to you and God for giving me a second chance to be your mother.*
>
> *"Sharon"*
> *excerpt from letter to child*

Just to give you a few examples, we have had men and women do everything from being extremely creative and painting a mural on a wall, to planting gardens, to writing a song, to buying a tiny teddy bear to sit on the nightstand. Make this memorial fit your talents and likes. This memorial also doesn't have to be anything you have to explain to people who come to your home. No one ever asks about the candle; it just looks like something I've put there for decoration. Also, you don't have to have this completed before you finish this class. But I would like for you to have an idea and know what you are going to accomplish.

Another nice thing is to share it with the class if you feel comfortable doing that. When you tell each other about your memorials, it's always fun and a very special time together when you see each other's talents and creativity.

**Write out some ideas for your memorial. Or if you know already what you're going to do, write it below:**

_____

_____

What if this child could talk to you? I want to share with you a letter that a lady going through the SaveOne class wrote. I think it is a fantastic mental picture of what Heaven is like and what he/she would say to the mom if he/she could.

*Dear Mama,*
*Just want you to know everything is fine. I'm sitting here in my usual place, resting in the arms of my dad in Heaven. He told me about your secret pain you have been carrying around for so many years of your earthly life. I don't quite understand what pain is, because here there is none. I don't quite understand what years are, because here there is no time.*

*Dad told me it was hard for you to ask my brother, Jesus, for forgiveness. I asked Jesus why you needed this "forgiveness". He said He didn't remember exactly what you did. He said something about the "sea of forgetfulness" is why He couldn't remember. He said He had this forgiveness for you even before you were born and that He was just waiting for your heart to take it.*

*He told me He lived for a while where you are now so He could make a way for you to come home. I asked Dad about the place you live. It sounds so different than here. He said He loves giving all His kids where you are presents. I have been noticing though that some kids don't like His presents, or they simply don't care to ask. He said it was because they were prideful and embarrassed. Those are awfully big words that I just don't understand. I asked Him why does He keep giving presents to kids who don't want them? He said because the kids ALL belong to Him and He wants to bring ALL of them home. He said He loves them no matter what. That I understand.*

*There are a lot of kids here that are just like me; just like there are a lot of Mom's where you are just like you.*

*I asked Dad in Heaven why you and me are apart from one another. He said He wanted to show the world His miracles, so He put you where you are to let everyone see what a miracle is. I think He called you His daughter of Amazing Grace, a child of His unconditional love. I guess you know by now my Dad in Heaven uses some pretty big words. Boy, when He speaks, things really happen!*

*I want you to know, Mama, that I'll always and forever love you because always and forever is what love is... and Mama, one last thing. I just want to say thanks for giving me a name to sign this letter.*

*Love,
Your daughter, Rachel Grace*

> Until now you have been a nameless, faceless part of my past. But tonight, I give you life by giving you a name and publicly acknowledging your presence in my life. God ushered you into His midst, an angel unforgotten, and it is with Him you will remain. While it has taken ten years for me to learn that I could love you, I promise now that I will never stop.
>
> "Bobbie"
> excerpt from letter to child

**What did this section teach you about this child?**

_____

_____

**What steps can you take this week to put this knowledge into practice?**

_____

_____

_____

**Write your memory verse for the week:**

_____

_____

*I recently had the privilege of speaking at a Right to Life annual conference. These are men, women, and teenagers who are working for the cause of life. They gathered from across their great state to learn, network, and be rallied to do more for the families being destroyed by choice.*

*After my talk that evening, many came over to my booth and asked me to sign their newly bought books. There was one man, in particular, I want to tell you about. He didn't buy a book, didn't ask me to sign anything, didn't tell me I did a good job, nothing. He simply wanted to tell me a story. His tale goes like this...*

*In 1975 he was a really good attorney by his own admission. He rarely lost any case he defended. One day a man called the attorney's office and said his wife had left him. He didn't want a divorce, especially now, because his wife had just told him she was pregnant... and getting an abortion. The caller asked the attorney if there was anything he could do to keep his child. This attorney told him there was no problem, that they would get an injunction against his wife to stop the abortion, and there was nothing to worry about. I could tell by the way this man spoke to me; he was very confident at the time that this child was safe by his actions.*

*The day in court came, and again my new friend, the attorney, had assured his client that all was well. As the judge began to look at the case, he asked the attorney to give him one law he could reference to uphold the injunction. And, of course, we all know now there isn't one.*

*Not. One.*

*Not one single law this attorney could find to save the life of this child for his client. His client was looking to him, and the attorney could do nothing. The pregnant wife's lawyer was there, and when she saw they could not uphold the injunction, she called the wife as she waited at the abortion clinic. She immediately went through with the abortion.*

As this attorney standing in front of me got to this part of the story, he broke down in tears, telling me that there was nothing he could do for his client and nothing he could do to save this child's life. He said, "I live with it every day."

Never, ever, ever fall for the lie that abortion doesn't have a ripple effect on many lives. 39 years later, and this man cannot tell the story without breaking down in tears. Abortion is a tragedy on many levels, created to divide, destroy, and bring death to millions. The tragic circumstance men face when trying to fight for the lives of their children is unconscionable and must be corrected.

What we have is the Truth that sets people free. With the overturn of Roe, I believe it is through abortion recovery we will make abortion unthinkable even before it becomes illegal in all 50 states.

Sheila

## JOURNAL PAGE

# CHAPTER 10
## *Brothers of Courage*

Verse to memorize this week:
*For God hath not given us the spirit of fear;
but of power, and of love, and of a sound mind.*

**2 Timothy 1:7**

As I prepared for this last chapter, I struggled with what example to use from God's Word regarding families or friends, and courage. I knew how I had admired the courage of each man and woman who works through this class, but I understood that you might not realize the magnitude of what you have just accomplished and how it can be used to help others. Work through this chapter, and let each story and each scripture sink in. Let what you have learned develop a steely resolve in your heart; and make a determination that you will never go back to the bondage you started out with weeks ago.

> *Courage is that quality of mind which enables men to encounter danger or difficulty with firmness, or without fear or depression of spirits... the highest degree of courage is seen in the person who is most fearful but refuses to capitulate to it.*
>
> *J. Oswald Sanders*

In *SaveOne - The Men's Study*, I use David as our example of great courage. In *SaveOne* for women, I use Esther as our example of great courage. But as I prayed and asked God about families, I was struck with Jacob and Esau. They experienced dysfunctional parents, being pitted against each other due to favoritism, deception, lying, a conniving mother, hatred, murderous intentions, and ultimately great forgiveness. It takes great courage to forgive great wrongs. Let's take a look at this story with fresh eyes.

Jacob and Esau were brothers. We read about them in **Genesis 25**. If you start in **Verse 28** you can read the whole story of how Esau sold his rights as the firstborn son to Jacob only for a paltry bowl of soup.

You may read that part of the story and want to scream, "WHAT WERE YOU THINKING?" However, isn't that something we all do on a regular basis? We sell our rights as a child of God for that indulgence into pornography, that piece of chocolate cake, just one more drink, and the list can keep going. We sell our rights all the time for stupid things that do not measure up. And of course, we can add to that list...abortion. Your friend or family member sold their rights of freedom and motherhood or fatherhood for what seemed to be the easy way out.

As we pick up this story in **Genesis 27**, we see how the conniving mother pits her sons against each other through deceiving their father. As a result the younger son received the one and only blessing their father had to give. Because of this, Esau develops a murderous hatred toward his brother Jacob and vows to kill him. Jacob's deception puts him on the run and for many years he and his brother are divided. The enemy loves when he can divide family and friends. He knows if relationships are divided, they are much weaker than when they are united. He is constantly prowling around looking for families he can destroy **(1 Peter 5:8)**.

Jacob lived for many years away from his family, isolated because of the poor choice he made that hurt his brother. He had to live wondering if around any corner, across the next hill, behind the farthest tree, a murderer who he once loved and played childhood games with was going to finally find him. Jacob built a fine life with many livestock, wives, and children.

When he knew he would have to travel near to where Esau lived, he sent a messenger with word to Esau asking him to be friendly to him. When we **read Genesis 32:6** we can imagine the fear that shot through Jacob's body when he learned Esau was already on his way to meet him with 400 men in tow. Scripture says Jacob was terrified! He starts making provisions to keep alive as many of his family and livestock as he can. We get an up close and personal view of Jacob's maturity that has developed through the years because the first thing he did was drop to his knees and pray. He asks God for safety and wisdom and reminds God of His promises.

Now let's back up just a minute in the story. Remember Jacob received the good blessing? Well, Esau received a blessing too.

**Read Genesis 27: 39-40.**

³⁹ Finally, his father, Isaac, said to him, "You will live away from the richness of the earth, and away from the dew of the Heaven above. ⁴⁰ You will live by your sword, and you will serve your brother. But when you decide to break free, you will shake his yoke from your neck."

That was the extent of Esau's blessing, just two short verses. Now it's the last part of Verse 40 that I want you to pay particularly close attention to. The New Living Translation of that verse reads, "...But when you decide to break free, you will shake his yoke from your neck." Could this verse be about forgiveness? Could Jacob have been prophesying that he knew the hatred rising up in Esau as he spoke? Such deception was committed against him; and by his own mother and brother! But Jacob suggests it would be up to Esau to decide when he would break free from this yoke of unforgiveness the enemy was placing around his neck.

Fast forward, and Jacob knows he is about to come face to face with the man he knows has wanted to kill him now for more than a decade.

**Read Genesis 33:4.**

⁴ Then Esau ran to meet him and embraced him, threw his arms around his neck, and kissed him. And they both wept.

My eyes fill with tears when I picture these brothers seeing each other for the first time in many years. God restored so much in these two and gave us an incredible look into their lives and how forgiveness and restoration ruled in the worst of circumstances.

Only God can bring about such things, and He can and will when we "decide to break free and shake the yoke from our neck." It was obvious by

Esau's reaction that he harbored no ill will toward Jacob. Even upon seeing all his possessions, he wasn't jealous. God had completed an awesome work, but it was up to Esau to receive it and allow the yoke to be removed.

> *Why should I fear? I am on a Royal Mission. I am in the service of the King of Kings.*
>
> *Mary Slessor beginning her remarkable missionary career in Calabar (now part of modern Nigeria)*

**Write your memory verse for the week:**
_____
_____
_____
_____

**This verse certainly describes Esau, doesn't it? But who else does it describe? Do you believe it describes you? Why or why not?**
_____
_____
_____
_____

**The word power could be translated into the word courage. Do you believe you have a spirit of courage? Why or why not?**
_____
_____
_____
_____
_____

**God also gave you a sound mind. Do you believe because of your courage to take this course your mind is more sound? Why or why not?**

_____
_____
_____
_____
_____

**Where did Esau get such courage?**

_____
_____
_____
_____
_____

In one part of the story, Esau is told when he decides to break free he will shake his yoke from his neck.

**What do you believe would have happened to Esau if he had never allowed himself the freedom to be released from this bondage?**

_____
_____
_____
_____
_____

That certainly would have been easier wouldn't it?

Read **Psalm 121**. Take each verse and, write in your own words what we're told about God and how He keeps us.

> *My abortion is no longer a secret. It is a mighty tool in the hands of a mighty God.*
>
> *"Jennifer"*
> *in SaveOne class*

**Verse 1:**

_____
_____
_____
_____

**Verse 2:**

_____
_____
_____
_____

**Verse 3:**

_____
_____
_____
_____

**Verse 4:**

_____
_____
_____

**Verse 5:**

_____
_____
_____
_____

**Verse 6:**

_____
_____
_____
_____

**Verse 7:**

_____
_____
_____
_____

**Verse 8:**

_____
_____
_____
_____

If we truly believe what this Psalm says, we will have the courage to do whatever God asks of us. We have to believe it though and put that belief into practice. Esau is a great example of having the courage to forgive and move forward in love knowing God will take care of the rest.

Because of Esau's actions, he paved the way for us to follow. He rose above the betrayal, the lies, the corruption, and dysfunction that marred his family.

He had every right to be angry and to live with a hefty amount of regret, but he chose to let it go. He realized carrying that burden was much more costly to him, his family, his future, and his relationships than breaking free from it would be. Making the decision to let it go paid off and he was able to experience a restored relationship.

> *For, while the tale of how we suffer, and how we are delighted, and how we may triumph is never new, it always must be heard. There isn't any other tale to tell, it's the only light we've got in all this darkness.*
>
> James Baldwin

Can you imagine what happened with both families as they watched these two brothers reconcile? Esau broke the cycle of dysfunction and hatred in his family for generations. We follow him through learning from his experiences. By his actions, he made it easier for us to believe we can accomplish the same things.

Throughout history, studies had been performed, and research conducted to conclude that man could not break the four-minute mark in the mile run. Experts told us it was a human impossibility to run a mile that fast.

He became the first man to ever break the four-minute mile.

Do you think Bannister just woke up one day and decided to break that record? No, he trained relentlessly for that day. But guess what has happened since Roger Bannister achieved his goal? More than fourteen hundred people have broken that same record after he paved the way. There were mental barriers that kept runners from believing they could ever achieve this record. But this one man set a new standard just because he believed he could. By his accomplishment, he broke down the mental barriers that stood in the way.

What courage it must have taken for this man to shun "fact" and believe he could do more. He discovered the impossibility to run a four-minute mile was really not a fact at all.

**Regarding your loved one's abortion experience, name something you believed to be fact, and now realize it is not:**

_____
_____
_____
_____
_____
_____
_____

**Read Luke 18:43. What happened to the blind man?**

_____
_____
_____

**Do you feel as though this is what has happened to you?**

_____
_____
_____
_____

**What took place when everyone saw the miracle Jesus performed?**

_____
_____
_____
_____

**What do you think would have happened if the man receiving his sight simply went into his home and told no one what Christ had done for him?**

_____
_____
_____
_____

It is only natural for you to want to tell others when something good happens. It's not always so easy when that something good involves being released from guilt, grief, or unforgiveness from a loved one's abortion. This is when we must draw from our source of courage.

**What is our source of courage?**

_____
_____
_____
_____

You may not have a desire to join us at SaveOne and start speaking in front of large audiences. We also don't suggest casually telling your co-workers or family about the past abortion. You have gone through some mighty changes, that doesn't mean all the people around you have also.

As a loved one of someone who has had an abortion, it really is not your place to tell others their story. You may have just experienced a wonderful time of allowing God's forgiveness to penetrate your own heart, or maybe you were released from unforgiveness you were harboring. You might have taken this class to try to come to grips with losing a child from your life you knew nothing about until after the fact. Whatever your situation, consideration must be thought out long and hard and a conversation needs to take place with the parent of the aborted child before you ever consider telling others what God has done for you in this class. Your loved one may still be reeling from their choice and is not able to face the aftermath just yet. Please respect your loved one's privacy by not telling others unless you have his or her permission and blessing.

> *I want to help others to have complete healing. No matter if it is one, two, or more. That sea of forgetfulness is big enough for them all.*
>
> *"Linda"*
> *in SaveOne class*

Allow God to use you when the time is right. I can't explain it, but it seems as though God steers the people to you who need to hear what He has done. We get calls all the time from men and women who have finished this book who tell us about being faced with the issue of abortion and being able to talk intelligently. Their old response would have been to run to the bathroom and cry or be extremely embarrassed. What we have found is the people who finish this book go back to their workplaces or homes and become the mother, friend, sister, or brother they were meant to be without all the emotional baggage abortion brought into the relationship.

**Write Psalm 30:6:**

_____

_____

The New Living Translation of this verse says, "Nothing will stop me now!" You have to have an unwavering determination that you will not be taken back to the place you were in before you took this class. Don't ever let Satan turn you back into a victim. You are a victor! Promise yourself that you will not look back, that you will always look ahead.

> *We are here to teach tomorrow's children through our experience, and God's merciful Grace. We are the missing arms of love, the missing voice of truth. It doesn't matter when we learned it or how long it took us to get to the place of today. Tomorrow's children are on their way here.*
>
> *"Brandi"*
> *in SaveOne class*

**Read Isaiah 43:18-19. What does Verse 18 tell you to forget?**

_____

_____

_____

_____

**What does Verse 19 tell you God will do for you?**

_____

_____

**If the relationship with your loved one is severed right now, do you believe God can restore it? Why or why not?**

_____

_____

**Read Ephesians 6:12-20.** Have a plan ready for when, not if, Satan attacks your mind and tries to make you remember things you believed surrounding the abortion situation. This is a battle you are in for your mind. Be immovable and believe that he will never win that battle again.

**Write out your plan of action to guard your mind against attack:**

_____

_____

_____

_____

> *The devil will give up when he sees you are not going to give in.*
>
> *Joyce Meyer*
> *Battlefield of the Mind*

**Read Philippians 1:6.** Don't let this be the end of the story. Continue on this journey of drawing closer to God and developing a deeper relationship with Him. Believe that God has started a work in you and will follow it to completion throughout your life.

I have one last bit of homework for you that is actually a challenge. My challenge to you is to SaveOne. Think of one person you know whom the effects of abortion have hurt. After preparing yourself through much prayer, draw from your source of courage and work to assimilate him/her into a SaveOne class. They may tell you no, and that's all right. God will do the rest. He will get the glory from your effort and your courage to step out and tell your story. Remember . . . Esau already paved the way.

**Write your memory verse for the week:**

_____

_____

No, dear brothers and sisters, I am still not all I should be, but I am focusing all my energies on this one thing: Forgetting the past and looking forward to what lies ahead, I strain to reach the end of the race and receive the prize for which God, through Christ Jesus, is calling us up to Heaven.

**Philippians 3:13–14.**

# JOURNAL PAGE

## JOURNAL PAGE

# IN CONCLUSION

Don't let your journey end here. Use the knowledge God has given you through this study to help others.

Please contact our office, and we will assist you in helping transform the lives of those who have been ravaged by abortion.

Be the willing vessel who will start a chapter of SaveOne in your area.

# SaveOne

**Helping men, women, and families recover after an abortion.**

At SaveOne, there is **ALWAYS** someone who cares.

Contact us for more information or to:
114 Canfield Place, Suite B-6 • Hendersonville, TN 37075
615-636-2654 • info@saveone.org • saveone.org

*Confidential appointments are available.
SaveOne is a non-profit organization.*

#lovelife

# OTHER BOOKS BY THE HARPERS

SaveOne: The Women's Study
(Sheila Harper)

SaveOne: The Men's Study
(Jack and Sheila Harper)

May I Have This Dance:
A Journal Through Pregnancy

Survivor:
My Journey Through Abortion and Back

Is There Not a Cause?
Your Battle Cry for Life

Finding You:
Recovering Your Identity After Sexual Trauma

Gifts from God
(Jack Harper)

Island Living: God's Plan to Rescue You from Isolation to Restoration
(Sheila Harper and Robin Gilliam)

My Sister's Keeper

My Sister's Keeper: Deep Dive Daily Devotional

**All books can be ordered by visiting SaveOne.org.**